SPORTS WRITER'S EYE

Also by Simon Barnes

Phil Edmonds: A Singular Man
Horsesweat and Tears
A La Recherche du Cricket Perdu
A Sportswriter's Year

SIMON BARNES

SPORTS WRITER'S EYE

AN ANTHOLOGY

Macdonald
Queen Anne Press

A Queen Anne Press Book

First published in Great Britain in 1989 by
Queen Anne Press, a division of
Macdonald & Co (Publishers) Ltd
66-73 Shoe Lane
London EC4P 4AB

A member of Maxwell Pergamon Publishing Corporation plc

British Library Cataloguing in Publication Data
Barnes, Simon
    Sportswriter's eye : an anthology.
    1. Sports
    I. Title
    796

ISBN 0–356–17914–1

Photoset in North Wales by
Derek Doyle & Associates, Mold, Clwyd
Printed and bound in Great Britain by
BPCC Hazell Books Ltd, Aylesbury, Bucks.

CONTENTS

INTRODUCTION

If you are a cub reporter on your first local paper, be very sure that the first thing to happen is that the Wise Old Sweat in the Newsroom will seek you out, breathe Guinness and Polos at you and start chuntering on about Tomorrow's Fish and Chip Wrappers. 'That's all it is. Don't get no fancy ideas, son.' Or love, or something worse, if the cub reporter is indiscreet enough to be female. If the reporter is a graduate, as he or she quite often is these days, the speech will include references to a graduate's supposed high-flown notions of literary worth. There's no room for that sort of thing here, you know. This is hard, this is brutal, this, son/love, is Real Life. A tough, no-nonsense stance is part of the great romance of newspapers. Their ephemerality only adds to the romance: you're only as good as tomorrow's piece, son/love. No one cares about what you wrote last week. It's not like *college* here. And the Old Sweat means that to sting, by God.

So here I am, strolling nostalgically through the streets of my past, searching the gutters for the wrappers of fish long dead, of chips long since eaten, a vinegar-scented pilgrimage to the shrine of my own ego. Such bliss! To collect the ephemera of recent years, so that it might be bound between covers, and be treated as a thing of permanent value! To be paid twice for all these pieces! Small wonder that I responded with glee when asked to be a part of this series of books, under the title of the *Sportswriter's Ego*. No, *Eye*, Freudian slip, but one in the eye for the Old Sweat, anyway. If he is alive today, he will be turning in his grave.

In truth, my past as a sportswriter doesn't take all that much strolling through. I've only been at it a few years. In a 'career' which some would call varied and others inconsistent,

1

wayward and dilettantish, I have never been a specialist in anything. However, after a long spell abroad, I returned to England to pick up the threads of the journalistic life, and within a few months found myself, to my immense surprise, writing about sport for *The Times*.

I owe this to Norman Fox, then sports editor on the paper, now deputy managing editor. I was a casual sub-editor at the time, going into the paper two or three days a week to work with the unsung heroes of journalism, the poor bloody infantry of the subs' desk. I wrote a piece for Norman on spec. I recall vividly the writing of it: shall I write in what I imagine is *Times* style? Then I thought, sod it. I'll take a punt, and write it the way I want to. The piece I wrote is the first in this selection, and after that, Norman Fox gave me more and more space and freedom over the next few years. Most people who have had any sort of luck in their working life will have someone to whom they owe a vast and forever unrepayable debt. Norman Fox is that man.

His successor, Tom Clarke, expanded my field still more, sending me away on aeroplanes, constantly encouraging me to follow my instincts rather than to live up to his own or anyone else's idea of what a sportswriter should do or be. And I have a licence to tease: sport is a great provoker of mirth. Frank Keating of the *Guardian* was a pioneer of funny and irreverent sports journalism, so there's another man in whose debt I stand. Humour doesn't preclude seriousness: it only precludes pomposity. That's the theory, anyway.

I have decided to present these pieces chronologically. It all seems to make better sense that way. Attitudes to issues, to places, and most particularly, to people, are always shifting and changing; people like Ian Botham and Steve Davis inspire a succession of responses. One December I wrote a serious piece of hagiography on Botham, the following February I became a hate figure among all England's cricketers and cricket writers for stating that Botham was a bit over-the-top. Only as good as your last piece, son. One year I wrote about how much I disliked Steve Davis. Later on, I was to find him one of the most fascinating characters in sport.

I have resisted the enormous temptation to rewrite all these pieces. There is less pure joy than one would think in contemplating the pieces of one's past. There is far more cringing than self-applauding involved. Oh my God, did I really write that? All these pieces are as they appeared in the paper, barring a few changes where errors occurred in transmission. I wanted to change far more than this, but I felt it would be too much like shooting a sitting duck.

Every Saturday, I write a column outside the sports pages. It appears opposite the page that carries the editorials and letters ('the Op-Ed page'). It is sort of a sporting diary, and its keynote is the humorous and the bizarre. I have interposed odd (some very odd) pieces from this column here and there, in an attempt to add yeast to the doughy mass of my longer pieces.

As I look over all these pieces, so representative of dedication worthy of a better cause, it is hard to escape the reflection that this is a very odd, and a very silly way of making a living. After all, not everyone believes that sportswriting is a respectable profession. There has always been a degree of intellectual snobbery surrounding sport. At school, it was the nitwits and the bullies who were keenest on sport. Me, I went to the pub and talked about James Joyce and D.H. Lawrence. Sport was beneath my lofty intellectual contempt.

These days, however, at least in my more optimistic moods, I incline to the view that sport is part of the whole person's approach to life. After all, even Joyce was fond of cricket, and included two pages on the subject in *Finnegans Wake*. Why should childish snobberies, and the antique division between the arties and the hearties, be allowed to spoil one's enjoyment of anything? Outside England, they have never heard of the arties and hearties problem. Samuel Beckett is the only Nobel Prize winner in the pages of Wisden; he bowled off-spin. Being a lapsed goalkeeper myself, I hold to the view that the true polymaths of history play in goal. Here, as proof of the fact that sport can be worth an intelligent person's time, I present my list of men of parts who have played in goal: my renaissance goalies. The collection includes Albert Camus, Vladimir Nabokov, Yevgeny Yevtushenko, Julio Iglesias, and the Pope. Indeed, it was Camus who once wrote: 'All that I know most surely about morality and the obligations of man, I know from football.' You can't argue with facts like that; let this be the book's epigraph.

Simon Barnes

PART 1

THE TIMES 1982-83

This is the first piece I wrote for *The Times*. At the time, my sister Julia trained a greyhound that ran at Henlow, and I had been there once or twice to make a donation to the Fund for Impoverished Bookmakers. She is one of the unnamed trainers I have quoted; not, I hasten to add, the one that calls the dog 'my baby'. I still have absolutely no idea what prompted me to suggest this as a suitable subject to write a piece about.

THROWING TO THE DOGS A BARE BONE CALLED HENLOW

December 1982

Henlow Greyhound Stadium is remarkable for its imposing atmosphere of brutal reality. It exists in a kind of microclimate, permanently 10 degrees colder than the rest of the universe, and rain seems never to settle on its surface, rather to howl parallel to it, propelled by knifing winds.

Henlow dog track appears to have a minimalist approach to sport: a bar, seven bookmakers, a totalisator and a sand track round which half a dozen lean dogs can provide a medium for a bet. It costs £1 to get in, including a racecard, the bookies pay a fiver to rent a pitch and in winter the 300 spectators at each meeting represent the hard core of greyhound loyalists.

It is basic stuff. One might expect the whole business to be a cynical benefit for hard-eyed manipulators, a haven for dopers, ringers and assorted fixers, as far from the ideals of Corinthian sportsmanship as it is from England's temperate climate.

But without wishing to portray Henlow as a corner of Bedfordshire peopled by gentle, dog-loving pixies, and without attempting to minimise the fact that the spectre of vaulting profit is a strong motivator at Henlow, as anywhere, there is a great deal more to it than that. As the greyhounds were going into the traps before a race a woman trainer declared, in a raucous, breathless voice: 'That's my baby out there!' 'Will he win?' 'I'll be happy if he just comes off sound ...' A stroll around Henlow's 'car park' is equally instructive: estate car after estate car. Because you need a bit of space at the back to keep your dog, don't you?

Henlow is a permit track. The racing is conducted under 'rules' – under the auspices of the National Greyhound Racing Club (NGRC) – which means, among other things, that 'permit trainers' can run their dogs there. And almost all Henlow's trainers are permit holders. There are 180 of them, and they pay £15 a year, plus £6 for each dog they train to a maximum of four. Small-timers, in short.

There are seven permit tracks among the 44 NGRC tracks in the country. The scheme is an effort to bring the small trainer into the NGRC fold. Without the permit scheme he would have to 'go flapping', or race his dog at a non-NGRC track, politely referred to as an 'independent' track. The difference between a 'rules' track and independent one is crucial: at a rules track the dog must race under its studbook name and therefore have a proper line of form in races and/or trials.

A permit trainer who usually races at Henlow said: 'I've taken my dog flapping a few times. You just make up any old name and if he's going well you can often pull off a win. But the bookmakers tend to be very wary and run a very tight book.' Everyone is betting in the dark at a 'flapper'; under rules, in theory, a shrewd investor can, if he wishes, make an intelligent assessment of the race. Henlow's racing manager,

John Smith, said: 'If a dog performs a long way off its true form it's my job to set up an inquiry. But at an independent track they just declare no race and all bets are void.' Smith, 30-ish and with a stylish taste in clothes, followed his father into the business. His father first leased Henlow in the early 1960s and ran it as a flapper; John Smith came into the family business like a Chinese No 1 son. Henlow became a 'rules' track in the mid-1970s and it is Smith's job to make sure that racing is fair, is seen to be fair and that his track makes money.

Profits come from admission, from across the bar and through the totalisator, which has a turnover of 'between £300,000 and £400,000' a year. Henlow keeps 12.5 per cent. As things stand, bookmakers cannot be charged more than five times the admission price to run a book and Smith believes that good bookmakers attract custom to the track. 'I would say that 99 per cent of the people who come racing at Henlow have connections with dog racing or with a particular dog,' he said. 'Of trainers, perhaps 20 per cent are in it for profit and nothing else. The rest are in it as much for the fun and satisfaction of running their own dog as for the chance of putting one over the bookies.'

It costs around £17 a week to keep a dog in training with a professional trainer affiliated to a leading NGRC track. It is cheaper for a permit trainer. One said: 'It costs me £8 a week to keep my dog in racing trim. That includes vitamins and, of course, a drop of sherry every day.' Smith said: 'At a small track you get involvement. A lot of trainers keep their dogs in the house as pets, always exercise them themselves, and the satisfaction of seeing your own dog win, when you've done all the work yourself, is tremendous.'

At the leading tracks the dogs seem sometimes like furry roulette balls. But a sense of closeness, of involvement, of brutal reality[1] makes Henlow a strangely pleasant place to spend an evening.

---

[1] Note the attempt to give the piece 'unity' by repeating a line from the first sentence in the last. It is a stylish trick of the writer who has run out of ideas.

I cut my teeth at *The Times* by writing a column called 'Outposts', in which I went to a series of minor and peculiar sporting events. This was a terrific notion, and one I enjoyed thoroughly. I have a macabre interest in darts, and so I went to watch the Great Man throwing arrows in a pub.

KING ERIC SHOOTS HIS ARROWS WITH THE MERRY MEN OF BOW

February 1983

As if being second in Bow and District Friendly League was not enough, that very night the sportsmen of the Freemason's Arms in Salmon Lane, E14 were about to welcome the greatest man in the history of their sport over the threshold. He was to step into the cockpit of competition and pit his mighty skills against those of the men of Bow and District.

There, beneath the clingfilm and the Bacofoil, lay the chicken legs, the cold sausages and French bread with which to do him honour. There, the sportsmen of Bow were limbering up, and playing practice games with an unconvincing attempt at insouciance. And at the end of the bar stood the landlord, Fred Lees, washing his hands with invisible soap in anticipation and standing, waiting, an imposing figure in his red woolly.

What was the time? If he didn't turn up in 20 minutes, he'd be late. The sportsmen drank more beer, and the air was full of a crackling sense of anticipation, as if waiting for the curtain to go up on a new Stoppard: would he really be as good as we all hoped? Would he come at all? If he did, would he be hideously and arrogantly late?

But punctuality is the politeness of kings, and this man was nothing less than kingly, albeit a king in mufti, as he arrived, shoving open the door of the saloon bar, uncontrovertibly and emphatically himself, golden lights in his hair, six foot two, with his smaller, blonder lady at his side, both wearing smiles, the king's gat-toothed and a mite off-straight.

'Anywhere I can change?' he asked. 'Then I'll come back and have a pint.' Have a pint! Did you hear that? He's a lad, isn't he? One of the boys all right. A tidal wave of nudges swept around the bar, and then, mere moments later, the king returned, this time in full regalia, the special shirt on his back, the ringing words 'Crafty Cockney' emblazoned thereon and Eric Bristow, the king of darts (for it was he) opened his throat and dispatched most of his pint of lager with an effortless swallow and started being pleasant to everyone.

'These magnificent athletes', as the inimitable Sid Waddell of the BBC called the legion of top flight darts players, earn their money in a bizarre way. Not for them the everyday turmoil of competition with their peers, the striving for victory every time they face their public. No, darts players earn the best part of their money from exhibitions; it costs at least £500 to hire Eric Bristow for the night, and perhaps £1,000 for major occasions, and for that money he will spend an evening throwing darts with stunning accuracy into any old dartboard in any old pub or club against any old opposition. It is as if racehorses spent non-racing days competing with the donkeys at Weston-super-Mare, as if Liverpool spent their lives playing teams from the gasworks, as if Muhammad Ali earned his real money by thumping old ladies in midweek.

Eric Bristow spends four or five, or more likely seven nights a week throwing darts, drinking lager and making nice with people. He can charge his five hundred quid minimum because he has proved himself just about the best there has ever been at throwing darts under pressure. But it is the daily grind of throwing and smiling that keeps the serious money rolling in.

'Course it's fun!' said Eric. 'Darts is always fun.' But what about the pressures of playing people who would sell their souls for a win over the king, what about the pressures of having to throw about 180s night after night, what about the fears of letting people down with a lousy night's throwing?

Well, our Eric is not a modest chap. Both an honest assessment of his own abilities and a nightly diet of defeating occasional dart-chuckers, militate against modesty. He just grinned at the dartboard and said with massive confidence: 'I won't let anybody down.'

Nor did he. He stood sideways on, the S-shaped nose pointing in predatory fashion at the target, his hand curved like a Thai dancer's in his eccentric praying mantis grip,[1] his hefty shoulder and upper arm so still they might have been resting on a plinth. The movement, which comes entirely from the forearm and wrist, acquires a grace oddly at variance with his bulky frame, and there is at once a considerable attraction in what he does, a fascination that comes from seeing any sportsman doing something quite extraordinarily well. Thunk – 60; thunk – 60; thunk – 60. A quiet smile of self-appreciation at the maximum.

'Well, it was always darts with him. And it was dedication that got him where he is today,' said Pam Bristow, Eric's mum. Eric's an East End lad, of course, and since his mum lives round the corner, it was only natural that she turned up as Eric's arrow-throwing rambles took him, for once, into wholly familiar territory.

'I used to work round here,' said Eric. 'In a cash and carry, when I was about 15. Bloody awful.' Gulp, swallow, an empty glass is refilled. 'What's that, love? Oh yes, I have been on a bit of a diet, but it's television, really; I look two stone heavier on television.' Excuse me Eric, a photograph, excuse me, Eric, could you sign this screwed up cigarette packet and write 'to Mavis' ... and Eric does it all with a will, and plainly earns every penny of that five hundred quid.

Maureen Flowers had been spelling him on the dartboard, giving the ladies a drubbing before Eric took on the men. She took a break and an orange juice ('darts players aren't all big drinkers you know'). She is the women's number one. 'I don't think the ladies will ever catch up with the men now,' she said. 'They've had so much exposure, they're all so used to television. We're not. We don't do as well as we should, I think the men have got too far ahead for us.'

At the board, yet another of Bow and District's finest sons

finds his game falling apart: 'Bottle job!' goes the cry. That's what the game is about, of course: the acquisition and retention of the mystical quality of bottle – nerve; lifting your game under pressure, refusing to crumble in a game wherein the most minute twitch of a finger muscle can influence a dart's flight and put it in the one bed rather than the 60. And Eric has confidence in bucketfuls, and more than mere confidence in his ability: Eric has confidence in his confidence, and that's something that makes him a very formidable adversary indeed.[2]

A new opponent from Bow: 'Come on, Killer!' cry the Friendly League colleagues in his support. 'You can do it mate.'

'Dedication,' said Eric's mum. 'As a boy he spent hour after hour throwing darts. He's never wanted to do anything else, and he's never really earned money doing anything else, except playing darts.'

Now he doesn't have to do anything else. Killer managed an 85, and left the board looking pretty pleased: Eric's arrows. Thunk – 60: thunk – 60; Eric turned to the crowd: 'Come on, Killer,' he shouted. The crowd roared: thunk – 60, hooray, hooray, well done Eric. And Eric takes another of those effortless swallows with an air of a man who has earned it. As for Killer, he won't forget the night he took on the king at 1,001 and lost by a mere 400 or so. And nobody has been let down. As Sid Waddell once said: 'Eric Bristow has put his darts where his mouth is.'

---

[1] Almost a mixed metaphor, but not quite, I think.
[2] Strange that some years later, Eric had a full year in which he suffered from 'dartitis', the dartist's equivalent of the yips, a nervous condition that made him unable to let go of the dart.

This is a truly silly piece of journalism. But its main fault is that it contains rather too many facts for my taste. The reason for this aberration is that I was given a lot of space for the piece. 'Don't cut any of the jokes,' I say to the sub-editors to this day. 'Cut the fact.' If there is one, of course.

PLAID! SHIRT! PER-TONK'S POCKETS OF CIVILISATION START THE BOULE ROLLING
May 1983

Dusty square, a dapple of sun. Clumps of people chatting and watching with idle interest. The steel boule arced through the air, bit the surface and rolled to within six inches of its target, the cochonnet, and guarded the approach. Alain St Denis haussed his épaules, and beamed: 'Like eet!' he said, and his captain agreed. 'Bloody good shot, Barbara,' he said, and Barbara Sharratt of the Wheatsheaf stepped from the circle. The pressure was all on Shedfield now.

The crowd was not sipping pastis, and very few were saying 'formidable'; it was pints of lager, nice one Mike, and to make things quite quintessentially English, at least one person in four was wearing a silly hat. The place was Southampton Sports Centre, the occasion the 10th British championships, sponsored by Piat, and the sport was pétanque, the francophile's shove-halfpenny. Anyone who has ever had cheese before the pudding knows this is the game played by French workmen, often in actual berets and blue overalls, outside cafés, in dusty squares beneath plane trees. It is a game watched with sleepy interest by a million tourists, drowsy after a carafe or two of déjeuner, lingering over a cup of coffee in the sun.

Most tourists seem to come home with a set of boules, for it is a well known fact that a holiday longer than a fortnight means you make a dozen vows to improve your life when you return, to make real coffee every time, to drink more wine and less lager, to be as civilised as actual Frenchmen who, after all, really do know how to live, don't they? Boules is a further symptom of capitulation to this pleasant myth, as everyone who has bought Pernod in preference to Scotch on the boat home well knows.

Just occasionally, the determination to amend one's existence takes a hold of someone with a sufficiently restless cast of mind to start using his filtre individuel. Maurice Adney-Hastings was just such a man, not content to leave his boules gathering dust beneath the stairs, nor to play occasional games in the back garden while he told stories about that awful waiter in Dieppe. At Sam's Hotel, Shedfield, he got British pétanque moving, and became founder president of the British Pétanque Association. What is more, the BPA has won international recognition.

When the world championships take place in Tunisia later this year, Britain will be there, and Stephen Lombard, aged 19 and with a vicious touch, will be fighting for Britain's honour. He plays regularly in Norfolk Square, the London spot for boules where French waiters and English enthusiasts chuck these cricket-ball sized cannonballs about with scientific zest.

'Britain's best so far was eighth place in the world championships, so my target is to improve on that,' said Lombard. 'I'll be going to Le Havre in June to get a lot of practice in.' He first got involved with the game when he was 12, learning, he explained mysteriously, in a French restaurant in Botley. He fancied the game, joined a club, and – voilà. 'I was impressed with the way he won his world championship place,' said Bob May, president of the Southampton Arms Pétanque Club. 'In fact, the bastard beat us to get there.'

But it is all serious stuff at the British championships, despite the silly hats, as the two teams of three battled it out in the final, fighting to reach the magic score of 15. There were four hats in evidence. Mike Sharratt, the Wheatsheaf captain, with an expressionless face and a murderous accuracy with his shooting, favoured a white hat like a largish *yarmulke*. Bob Britton, captain of the opposing Shedfield side, preferred a John Lennon nostalgia peaked number, while his colleague, Terry Bill, wore a Lady Di floppy tweed job. Philip Deane wore a stable lad's flat cap, but removed it when he got down to business.

It worked, too. A rogue boule from Shedfield wormed its way through the Wheatsheaf's guard and gave them a single point for the first end, the scoring being like the English game played on green stuff. Wheatsheaf hit back with two from the next end and three from the third. 'Shirt!' said M. St Denis. 'C'est bien joué, hein?'

May of the Southampton Arms was acting as interpreter of the game's finer points. 'The main difference between bowls and pétanque, apart from the throwing technique, is that shooting, or firing as they say in bowls, is more unusual in the lawn game. In pétanque, you'll get several attacking boules in every end. In fact, the ultimate shot in pétanque is the carreau. That's the 180 of the game, when you aim at your opponent's boule and clout it miles away, while your own stops dead in its place.'

Shedfield clawed their way back into the reckoning, and trailed 5–4, and Wheatsheaf were under threat. It was time for drastic measures: M. St Denis took a Gaulloise from his pocket and lit it. No English player could fail to be intimidated. Wheatsheaf drew away again, to 7–4, but with Britton polishing his boules on his corduroy trousers like Dennis Lillee, Shedfield drew level after an error from the Frenchman. 'Oh byang jeway, Alain,' barracked a copain from the sidelines.

There are pockets of pétanque all over Britain, clubs in Scotland and Wales. In Southampton, there are four municipal pétanque terrains. A terrain must be flattish and grassfree, preferably dusted with very fine gravel. Breweries can sometimes be cajoled into laying out the £500-odd you need to establish one at the pub. A set of boules bought in England will cost around £16, but a magic set for the soi-disant master will set you back £24. The British Pétanque Association (nothing fancy about them, they pronounce it 'per-tonk') is fussy about its boules. They must be stamped with both serial number and weight, otherwise they are 'dog boules' and suitable only for a back garden jolly.

But merde, what is this? A daring placement of cochonnet into a freakish little gulley in the terrain. 'Your terrain needn't be perfectly flat,' May explained. 'That's where a little extra skill can come in.' He has reason, this man. Wheatsheaf went in one end from 8–7 to 11–7, with a couple of needle-threading boules from Mike Sharratt. 'Plaid!' said M. St Denis.

The youngest player at Southampton was Ian Barnett, holding his own in good company at the age of 10. His brother, a 13-year-old, hammers all the best at the Fountain Inn and has won the soubriquet of Mark the Shark.

Shedfield, faces grimmer by the minute beneath their chapeaux, laboured back to 11–11, but some clever stuff from the Frenchman pegged them back again: 13–11. A new end, the last? Barbara Sharratt set a hot pace with a finely judged opener which the Shedfield men were never able to match. Mike Sharratt stepped to blast their best effort to one side. 'Shirt!', and it was all over. Wheatsheaf were champions, and the teams exchanged handshakes and kisses.

A frightfully civilised afternoon. 'Some French people I've stayed with refuse to play the game because it is too low class for them,' mused May. 'But over here, it's all doctors and architects, and businessmen.' C'est drôle, hein? But maintenant for un pint de lager.

In the autumn, I took on a project of following the FA Cup from first qualifying round to final. Many a journo has trodden this route, Brian James with the most distinction. It was a good and an educational experience. I have always loved non-League best in football. This was the first piece in the series: Uxbridge v Chalfont St Peter.

FROM THE WASTELANDS TO GLORY
September 1983

Honeycroft! Something of a misnomer, I fear, for this was no lush pasture in some gentle combe. Picking my way through a wasteland of scrub and rubble, past various heaps of broken images, I felt more like Neil Armstrong than a man off to watch a cup match. Not just any game, either. This was the FA Cup and though you might think that the cricket season has hardly stopped and that you won't have to worry about the FA Cup until January, life is very different for the men of Honeycroft.

On Saturday, the first qualifying round of the FA Cup was played, and 288 clubs were playing for their lives, honours and a couple of quid bonus. Eighty-two of them had already gone through the preliminary qualifying round, among them Chalfont St Peter, who dismissed Finchley 2–1. This was something of a worry for Uxbridge, the bold boys of Honeycroft field, for they had been turned over by the odd goal the previous Saturday by none other than Finchley. Uxbridge share the London borough of Hillingdon with three other senior clubs, and are in their second season of Isthmian League football. Chalfont St Peter are in the Athenian League, and come from what they claim is the largest village in England.

There are 488 clubs in the FA Cup this year. Twenty élite non-League clubs are invited in at the fourth qualifying round, after which comes the first round proper, and the entry of the Third and Fourth Division clubs. 'Every small club like ours hopes for a little run in the FA Cup, playing for the chance of meeting a Football League club. It is a question of cash – and glory,' said an Uxbridge committee member, Alan Odell.

Uxbridge have played in every FA Cup since the competition started and that, as every reader of teatowels knows, was in 1871, the competition which ended when Wanderers beat Royal Engineers 1-0 at Kennington Oval. Uxbridge have not made the first round proper for many a long year, but they did play England at Wembley in 1976 in a practice match. England won 8-0, and of course, there is a big picture of the occasion in the boardroom, along with many pictures of sepia-tinted glories, calf-length shorts, moustaches like bayonets and goalies with caps the size of soup tureens.[1]

Chalfont St Peter won the Athenian League Cup last year and, after their defeat of Uxbridge's recent conquerors, clearly had a decent chance of getting through to the next round. But as their chairman, Ted Brown, said: 'Realistically, we know we won't get far in this competition. It is not the be-all and end-all for us; in fact the FA Vase, where we have a real chance, is more attractive. But our major concern is a good League position, because we want to move up to the Isthmian League.' Indeed, Uxbridge themselves clambered from the Athenian League into the fresh air and sunlight of Isthmian League Division Two, consolidating a position they had worked to establish for many years, involving buying a new ground for £125,000, spending £50,000 on improvements, and what is more, remaining in the black.

Before the match, the fruit machines burped and swallowed, and so did the men in the bar, having one last before the kick off, and that, of course, is how the money comes. Gate receipts cover the fees for match officials on a good day. The teams emerged and the drinkers followed, walking across the grass at a 45-degree angle as the wind swept unmercifully across the badlands of West Drayton. Roger Nicholls was in goal for Uxbridge, playing his 705th game for the club – he has missed six games in 10 years and he won't get dropped next week, either, because he made a couple of cracking saves straight away, defying Chalfont's traditional version of the controversial temperamental skills-merchant, one Steve Smith.[2]

'Go, go, go, lads, we've *gotter* believe in it,' the Chalfont players were shouting in the second half, 2-0 down after Williamson and Church had struck. Jackett demonstrated his belief by pulling a goal back from a free kick, but Duff, who has the plum job of principal striker for Uxbridge (86 goals in three seasons) made it 3-1. All over for the gallant Saints?

That would be a slur on the good name of Chalfont: Smith got the goal his skills deserved, his side remembered it was a

Cup tie and it was all grand stirring stuff, with Chalfont having the better of things, and Elderfield rumbling out of defence to clout a very pleasant volley that near broke the crossbar. 'Blow the whistle, ref, the bar's open,' came the swelling voice of the 150-strong crowd, anxious for safety and Scotch. But Duff scored one for the road to make it 4-2 for Uxbridge, and perhaps that will make Hampton think a bit. Hampton, 7-1 conquerors of Leyton-Wingate, face the rigours of Honeycroft in the next round on 1 October, as indeed do I.[3]

Ron Clack, the Uxbridge manager, was happy with the goals. 'All good footballing goals. We play a lot of one-touch in practice and it is nice to see it come off in a match.' He has managed the club for 14 years and lives in a flat over the clubhouse at Honeycroft. And he is quietly hopeful of the chances against Hampton. After all, by then his centre-back will be back from his holidays in Italy.

[1] A serious case of overdoing the similes here.
[2] What do you mean, *one* Steve Smith?
[3] The boys of Honeycroft got stuffed.

Bicycle polo is probably the silliest sport in the history of the world. This I present as the summit of my achievement as a minor sports correspondent.

A TOUCH OF IRISH IN A GAME SO ECCENTRICALLY ENGLISH
September 1983

Bicycle polo was once an Olympic sport, so let us have no unseemly mockery of the nine teams who recently trekked across England to thrash and pedal for the George Brake Trophy at Purley Way playing fields. The twinkle-kneed brotherhood may have looked a trifle incongruous as, knees going like berserk pistons, they flung themselves into the fray on a pitch surrounded by football fields and Sunday afternoon George Bests, but they were playing a real sport with honoured traditions.

The rain was coming down in great sheets while players between games in this round-robin tournament stood around in anoraks and bedewed spectacles, fiddling with bikes, talking bicycle polo shop or pedalling about practising telling passes. 'Not me,' said The Maltese Cat. 'I don't race. I play the game.' But unlike the equine game, a game in which running a team costs as much as running an ocean-going yacht, I am told, bicycle polo is cheap. A polo bike will cost a mere £89.

The sport is in the middle of rescuing itself from an all-time low, with membership of the Bicycle Polo Association (BPA) hitting unplumbed depths three years ago. But at Purley, Chelsea Pedlars turned up, a newly registered outfit with an impressive 42 playing members. They had been going for three years outside the fold, but now they were contesting the George Brake Trophy for the first time, with public school accents and one player wearing, for reasons best known to himself, a pair of real jodhpurs.

'Basically it all started as a hare-brained scheme dreamt up in a pub,' explained the Chelsea captain, Nick Mayhew-Sanders. Joe Garnett, a player with a silken kerchief about his head, added: 'We play because it really is great fun. We use smaller mallet heads than most of the players here, and the ball rises something wicked. That tends to keep the adrenalin flowing.' They play twice a week, more often than most of the more experienced players, and have a pitch in Hyde Park.

But experience and technique count in this game, a strange sport that demands strange skills. 'I'm a newcomer,' said Clem Cowling, a slip of a youth somewhere in his 60s. 'I didn't start playing until 1947.' He was playing at back for Crystal Palace, much to his surprise he was co-opted into the side after he had turned up to watch. They were going rather well, as it happened. 'Of course, in the old days Palace were the old enemy,' he said. 'I used to be with Croydon Aces, you see.'

This is, indeed, a long-established sport. In fact, it is

probably the only sport to have been invented twice. Perhaps not altogether surprisingly, it was invented by an Irishman first time around: Richard Mecredi was a racing cyclist too old for the road and so, like The Maltese Cat in the Kipling story, he started to play the game, pausing only to invent it. That was 1891, and to this day, Ireland are the world's only Olympic gold medal winners in the sport of bicycle polo. That was in 1908, when the Olympic Games were held in Shepherd's Bush.

But Cyril Scott was unaware of these fascinating facts, and so he invented the game again, and founded the BPA in 1930. The game spread rapidly, through many cycling clubs packed with enthusiastic racers happy to find a winter way of keeping fit. 'I started in 1933,' said Fred Bull, while Chelsea A were in the process of getting thumped by the accuracy and skill of Solihull. 'I played for Wandsworth in the London League days, after the war, when we used to play in greyhound stadiums, and get crowds of 2,000. George Brake was the man behind it, of course. He tried to organise the sport on a semi-professional basis, but the crowds were never quite big enough. I don't play any more though, not since I broke my wrist falling off a mountain.'

The BPA secretary, Tony Knight, remembers playing his first game on an errand boy's bike with a basket on the front, but a proper polo bike is a specialist machine, with extra strong wheels, a contorted frame and straight front forks which make the turning circle as small as possible; no brakes, a fixed wheel, and an extremely low gear that makes for rapid acceleration, and means that travel at any speed is an irresistibly comic sight. The bikes also have tiny handlebars 'so you don't rupture yourself in a sudden turn,' Mr Knight explained kindly. You buy your mallet from Salters, who also make the mallets you use when you play bicycle polo on horseback.

Or elephant back ... the Mounted Sports Association of India, whose members play polo on bikes, horses and elephants, recently toured England: 'all maharajahs and princes. They beat us 10-5,' said Mr Knight. Chelsea Pedlars also played them and, like Mr Knight's boys, were invited to

India to play. Chelsea think they might actually make it in February.

And think not that bicycle polo men are cissies. It is a game that can be exuberantly physical, and a passing movement can leave a wreckage of bikes, mallets and limping players in its wake. 'I like the game because it is quick, with plenty of aggression and skill,' said Robert Walker, the captain of Solihull and England. In the last international, two years back, Scotland beat England 5-3.

Clem Cowling helped the old enemy, Crystal Palace, to third place while Mr Knight lifted his team, Solent B, into fourth. The final was played between Bec and Solihull, and Walker, lining up for the Solihull side with his sons Mark and Adam, won 4-2 after extra time. It is true that Purley Way playing fields are a long way from the Olympic Games, but there will always be an England so long as bicycle solo is played as a serious sport.

From the Diary

Russian gymnast Olga Korbut had a secret vice which can now be revealed: a penchant for English beer. Needless to say, satisfying it was strictly against the rules, but at competitions she would sit next to a sympathetic British official who would order a pint and put it in front of him. Olga, eyes darting hither and thither for danger like an antelope in the Serengeti, would surreptitiously knock it back.

I was now getting about to interview real sportsmen, and real stars. So naturally I wanted to interview Frank Worthington. Frank: the superstar that never was, but really should have been.

WORTHINGTON BEING FRANK ABOUT PELÉ, ELVIS AND HIMSELF
November 1983

Joe Mercer talks about him in the same breath as Pelé and Dixie Dean. Lawrie McMenemy talks about him in the same breath as the giant panda. There is no doubt that Frank Worthington is one of the more extraordinary players in the First Division. 'Well, he could play, couldn't he?' said Mercer, who picked Worthington as centre-forward in his delightful short period as England manager between the method eras of Ramsey and of Revie. 'He's one of a dying breed, and you've got to look after people like that,' said McMenemy, the manager of Worthington's current club, Southampton.

Worthington has scored 196 League goals, and wants to make it 200 before his 35th birthday, which is on 23 November. But what's the best goal you've ever scored, Frank? He's got it on video: edge of the box, back to goal, bouncing the ball twice on his foot and then as three defenders surge in on him, he flicks it over his head, turns and volleys in. Whack. Sublime.[1]

'When I was a kid, I had a white plastic football, and I played with it every day until it got dark. Then I used to play under a gas lamp. Then I went to bed and dreamed about football. I used to play keepy-uppy, all that sort of thing. You become the master of the ball. That's not something that's encouraged today, especially not at junior level. They teach kids to run all day instead, the worst thing they can do. They don't teach the finer points of the game. Don't even teach the three basics: control, passing, and shooting. And so everything becomes rigid and sterile. Sure, fitness is important, but the bottom line is skill.

'Look at that now. Or that,' Pelé is on the video now, a tape that has been played and played till it is almost transparent, and Worthington knows every frame. 'What a man. A genius. Never be another Pelé, the way there'll never be another Presley.'

Worthington still gets called 'Elvis', and as ever, wears his hair in a coal black Presleyesque mane. You still hear occasional stories of Frank pulling out a comb on the pitch. Such tales are flagrantly untrue, but the fact remains that the idea of big Frank, with his cad's moustache, pulling the ball down and volleying into the net while teasing his quiff into shape is irresistibly attractive. 'I suppose there is something a little showbiz about the way I play,' he said. 'Entertainment, live bands, theatre, cabaret, are a big part of my life. I like to be entertained and I like to entertain.'

But apart from his eight internationals, Worthington has never played on a really big stage. He is a much travelled man, whose past clubs are Huddersfield Town, Leicester City, Bolton Wanderers, Birmingham City, Leeds United and Sunderland – hardly giants. Bill Shankly came within a whisker of buying him for Liverpool, but pulled out when a medical examination revealed blood pressure problems. The problem was temporary; its result permanent: 'It didn't seem all that important at the time, but now I know that if I had gone to Liverpool I wouldn't have won eight caps. I'd have won 88. But I'm a fatalist. It all comes out the way it is written – and besides, I've enjoyed it. Especially the two years at Bolton.' He won the Second Division championship medal in the first season at Bolton and the Golden Boot award for being the First Division's leading scorer with 24 goals, in his second.

'He is one of the best English centre-forwards of all time,' said Mercer. 'And he's a lovely man. If the stands were falling down round his ears, he'd play. He is a target, you can hit him and the ball sticks. He gives you time. He's got confidence. You can build teams round him. But Revie and Ramsey never fancied him. I just couldn't understand it.'

Well, Worthington is flash. He unconsciously does simple things with extreme grace; consciously he loves to put on a show. 'But I'm not an out and out individualist like Rodney Marsh. I've always worked to use my talent for the benefit of the team.'

'He's only got one goal this season but I'm not bothered about that,' said McMenemy. 'He's a target; he adds experience to a front line with youngsters Wallace and Moran.'

'All spectators love to see skill,' said Worthington. 'But it gets eased out, because of the systems, the faceless teams. Dave Mackay said that the systems were just ways of covering up weakness, and he was right. Football has gone backwards since we won the World Cup, lost the characters and the individuals with skill. The systems have taken over.'[2]

Worthington is a man who does not quite fit into the systems. He must play for a team in his own way. He can't bear to be boring. He can make the game look both easy and fun. 'I know it sounds silly,' said McMenemy. 'But he likes playing football.' No wonder Frank Worthington is an anachronism.

---

[1] I saw it on television again the other day. It looks better than ever.
[2] The relationship of individual skills to a team is something that has always fascinated me: flair against competence, inspiration against perspiration — these are matters I shall return to. Ah me, où sont les Worthingtons d'antan?

PART 2

THE TIMES 1984

Here is another footballing man with a bit of class to him. I wrote a series of four pieces about goalkeepers, but Bruce Grobbelaar was my favourite. When I was a goalie, I played in the Grobbelaar way. But I lacked his quality of reliability.

A KEEPER THROWS UP HIS HANDS IN LAUGHTER AT HIS MISTAKES

March 1984

Bruce Grobbelaar, the Liverpool goalkeeper, was lucky he did not get sent off in the Milk Cup final last year, when Gordon McQueen, of Manchester United, broke through only to go down with the onrushing Grobbelaar in a great tangle of limbs. It was a time when sending keepers off was the trendy thing for referees but Grobbelaar escaped with a booking. Then there was the match against Widzew Lodz when Grobbelaar dropped a cross trying to make a one-handed catch and Liverpool promptly lost the European Cup.

Talking about mistakes requires delicate conversational footwork when you are talking to a goalkeeper. Peter Shilton is coldly self-accusing, analytical, determined to work still harder, to train and train until no error is ever possible again. But Grobbelaar roars with laughter. 'You thought I was bad against Widzew Lodz? You should have seen me against

Nottingham Forest last time. I was even better – I didn't do one thing right. Every cross, I dropped it. Every shot, I fumbled. The ball was a bar of soap, my hands were covered in lather. They didn't score – but I don't know how.'

Perhaps Grobbelaar doesn't take football with the kind of Shanklyesque seriousness you would expect from the Liverpool goalkeeper. All newspaper readers will understand why, for they know the relief of turning from the turbulence of the foreign pages to the cheering trivia of the sports section.

Grobbelaar was for two years a foreign page statistic instead of a sports section name; at the age of 17 he was involved in the guerrilla war in what was then Rhodesia. He believed with utter certainty that he was going to die. Such things put football in perspective. His time, spent in tracking units, was made doubly horrific by the authentic Catch-22 extension of his service: he was called up for a year at 17, told to do another six months, then six months more. He was dropped by helicopter into the middle of the fighting. So what does a dropped football matter, even if it does cost Liverpool the European Cup? 'I just thank my lucky stars I'm still here,' he said. 'I came out of the Army knowing I was good enough to do anything I desired.'

What Grobbelaar desired was to play football again. He comes from a goalkeeping family: his father kept goal in an international, his mother kept goal in hockey. Grobbelaar set off as a peripatetic goalkeeper, playing in South Africa, training in England (with West Bromwich Albion), but failing to get a work permit, playing in Vancouver, then getting a work permit to play for Crewe at the bottom of the Fourth Division and finally signing for Liverpool. Bob Paisley, the Liverpool manager, went to watch Grobbelaar at Crewe and made his mind up during the kickabout.

Then Liverpool's first choice goalkeeper, Ray Clemence, left to go to Tottenham Hotspur and Grobbelaar was suddenly number one keeper for the country's number one team. In football it is standard practice to keep the uncompromising professionals at the back. If you have any oddballs at all, you play them at the front. But Liverpool, the ultimate professionals, plonked this gangling extrovert, with his cartwheels and his handstands in the goalmouth, right in the key position.

English resistance to the flashy guys is traditional, especially among journalists. When a Bowles, a Best or a Hudson has a lapse it is an indictment of the entire concept of being flash. When the flash guy in question is a goalkeeper and his error costs a goal – well, it is open season. 'A goalkeeper must learn to be critical of his own performances, he must know when he is in the wrong,' Grobbelaar said. 'But I hate it when I've had a moderate day and the Press tell me I've had a stinker. Journalists don't think I'm good because I'm flashy. But I don't think they would treat an English player in the same way.'

Grobbelaar has stunning natural ability as a shot-stopper and that was the quality that caught Colin Addison's eye in South Africa. Addison, now managing Newport, had much to do with Grobbelaar's trips to England and then to Canada. 'His agility is quite remarkable,' Addison said. 'So is his physique. He is an imposing character, with good hands. And he's becoming a better keeper all the time as he adds knowledge of angles and timing to his abilities as a shot-stopper.'

However, Grobbelaar is known more for his errors than for his abilities: the word 'eccentric' has become his very own journalistic cliché, his mistakes always attributed to 'rushes of blood'. Grobbelaar continued: 'A Liverpool goalkeeper has to be a sweeper as well as a goalkeeper. When the Liverpool defence gets caught I have to come off my line. The fault is not that I go for a ball when it beats the defence. The fault is the occasional split-second hesitation.'

Many people still find it hard to believe that Liverpool, of all clubs, have signed that 'eccentric' goalkeeper. Such opinions leave Liverpool sublimely unconcerned, of course; they have just given Grobbelaar a new three-year contract.

From the Diary

The passing of Lillee and Chappell does not mean the loss of all that's most endearingly Australian from sport: witness the recent All-Australian Beer Belly Competition, won by Gordon Mather. Presenting the prize – 120 bottles of beer – a politician called Russel Hinze said: 'You can tell they're not bloody queers.'

The Boat Race has always been a particularly Timesian sort of event. Here is a piece with Daniel Topolski, who is one of those sporting polymaths I hold so dear. It is also a piece about arties and hearties, part of the same long debate. Topolski coached Oxford through a long winning streak, leaving them after the bizarre 'Boat Race Mutiny' in 1987.

MAVERICK MAKING A NAME BY TEAMWORK
March 1984

Those people who find it surprising that someone so extrovert as Dan Topolski should be in charge of the Oxford Boat Race crew are not really concentrating. Enjoyment and appreciation of the maverick is a traditional part of English life. The more proper the organisation, the more tolerance there is for the chap who does not quite fit into it. The lad who reads Keats behind the cricket pavilion is no rebel but is conforming to a part of the English heritage.

Topolski, the son of the artist Feliks, has a natural genius for not fitting in. He first rowed in the Boat Race in 1967, the year, significantly, of *Sergeant Pepper's Lonely Hearts Club Band*.

The prevailing chic, in Oxford and the world, was all to do with sex and drugs and rock and roll, hair down to your feet was *de rigueur*, and the only thing totally, I mean *totally*, uncool was getting heavy about sport. Topolski rowed in the Blue boat despite being far too light and far too cool to be taken seriously as an oarsman, and also made it in the appropriate radical chic circles despite coming out of the closet as a heavy sporting dude. 'When I made the Oxford crew, I had to go public,' Topolski said. 'It was a shock to some people.'

Topolski has had more to do than anyone else with the recent dominance of Oxford in the Boat Race. In 1972, he reorganised, changed emphasis and co-ordinated the efforts of the four or five coaches who trained the Blue boat. 'But I don't feel I'm a top-class coach. Because I've got so many interests, I tend to devote less time than I could to rowing.'

Like the other coaches, Topolski is an amateur. His true profession is perhaps most exhilaratingly described as adventurer: he is a professional larger-than-life character, involved with writing, television, a maker of spectacular journeys of the overachieving kind. He is the renaissance man of rowing, and looks like a Bronzinian cherub who has been going through a really hard time.

The legend of his journey through Africa, in order to become appropriately Topolskian, has become a saga of unimaginable privations and exertions. The exaggeration to mythic proportions is hardly his doing; it is just the kind of stuff that accumulates around Topolski, a man whose breadth of horizon makes a nice change from footballers who see Birmingham as a challenge.

'I lost my chance of going to the Olympics in 1972 by going to Africa. In 1976, I blew it again by going to the Hindu Kush. I hate choices. I always try to do them both. In 1978, I was in the Great Britain lightweight crew. We all wanted a gold medal in the world championships. Then I was offered a chance to sail with Clare Francis. But this time I thought: No, I want a medal. We won it by six inches.'

However, Topolski the ramblin' man and Topolski the sportsman are far from incompatible. Rowing, he said, has been the thread of discipline running through his life, an obsession he is able to pick up and put down again. The professional adventurer will march on: 'I couldn't be a professional coach – that's an awful thought. I've got other plans for myself. I've no idea what they are, but I've got other plans ...'

From the Diary

The Hong Kong Chinese call Europeans *gwai-lo* or ghost people, because of their pale skins and other ill-omened attributes. In deference to the Chinese love of puns, a team of European footballers from the outlying island of Lamma have called themselves *Gwai-loong* or ghost dragons, a rough translation being 'Super Wogs'. They are acquiring sponsored kit, but continue to play all in white. For the Chinese, white is the colour of funerals and death. 'It gives us a vital psychological advantage,' says their player-manager, John Kier.

Here is a piece on Phil Edmonds, the former England bowler and misfit. This was the first time we met; I got to know him pretty well, because he was the subject of my first book, a biography called *Phil Edmonds: A Singular Man*. This interview took place just after he had been dropped once again. But he was on the verge of forcing himself back into the side as a fixture. After this piece appeared, Edmonds was ordered to make a public apology to Mike Brearley.

THE AWKWARD LEFT HAND OF ENGLAND
May 1984

I'm not saying that Phil Edmonds is a particularly competitive guy, but on the other hand, how many cricketers appeal every time the ball passes the bat? I mean, in the nets? Edmonds, a left-arm spinner with Middlesex and sometimes with England, has managed to reserve for himself the title of the most awkward person in cricket (and the competition is not negligible). When I asked how it all happened, he showed complete bewilderment. For in fact Phil Edmonds is the nicest guy in the world – I know, because he told me so himself.

But last summer you could hear the relieved sighs of the cricketing establishment being heaved the length and breadth of the country when Nick Cook turned in such excellent bowling figures after a back injury had forced Edmonds out of the England side. Thank God, they all thought. Now we won't have to take Edmonds on tour. In fact, trying to put together an England side or touring party without bringing in the stately, upright left-arm spin of Edmonds has been a conundrum that has vexed the minds of the mighty for years. The Australian touring party that contained three off-spinners might have been deliberately selected to ram home the apparent official point of view: if you can tweak the ball a bit and your name isn't Philippe Henri Edmonds, you're in with a chance.

Last summer Edmonds forced himself back into the England side by taking bags of wickets in June. 'I'd quite like to embarrass the blighters into picking me again,' he says. 'I mean, the only top-rate spinners in the country are me and Embers.' And John Emburey, Edmonds' Middlesex colleague, is still unavailable for England selection after going to South Africa.

It is the Edmonds attitude that gets the blame. 'Easy to get a reputation. Impossible to lose it. I just have to make a *suggestion* these days, and it is interpreted as being antagonistic.' The reputation for awkwardness is not a new one: he acquired the dressing-room nickname of Maggie when Mrs Thatcher was Leader of the Opposition.

'It's amazing how I've acquired the reputation of being the one they want to leave out. I wonder how it all happened...' Well, his relationship with the Middlesex and England captain, Mike Brearley, was not exactly irrelevant. 'I got on the wrong side of Brears. I'm the sort of guy who needs a man's man to hit me on the head when I step out of line. But Brearley was too namby-pamby, too schoolmasterly. He has this need to dominate the dressing-room intellectually – in the same way that Ian Botham needs to dominate a dressing-room physically. And I didn't knuckle under to Brearley. Maybe I should have done.'

Edmonds was at one stage the vice-captain of Middlesex, and the likely successor to Brearley. It didn't work out quite like that. 'Brearley manipulated for two years to get me out of the vice-captain's job.' Mike Gatting got the captain's job, a cricketer who, Edmonds believes, would play much better for England without the inhibiting presence of Botham ... though Edmonds also says he is a Botham fan and mate.

Edmonds is not wholly complimentary about today's crop of Test match cricketers: 'We have a mediocre Test side and the reason is that selectors have consistently gone for malleable mediocrity. Test match cricket today is born out of terror, the terror of losing.' He believes a Test side should have two, yes two, spinners and three seamers (one bowler being an all-rounder), five specialist batsmen and a glove-man. 'I felt for Cooky last winter, a spin bowler on a tour dominated by terror that the batting would fail. Packing a side with batters doesn't help.'

Edmonds has a terrific knack for getting on the wrong side of important people. There was that wigging from Peter May after he was reported for his 'sledging' of Vengsarkar ('All I said was "Never mind, Dilip, it's only a Test match" '), and then that ludicrous pair of bouncers he bowled at Hadlee last summer, final proof for many that Edmonds could never be properly trusted to be a sensible Test match cricketer. 'There's too much seriousness in cricket,' Edmonds said.

Now, he says, his problem is motivation. Trying to force the blighters to pick him may not be spur enough, he fears, as rising business interests get in the way. He is 33 and this season could be the last. 'I'm frustrated that I have not fulfilled my potential as a cricketer.' The constant frustrations of being the official awkward guy of English cricket have got to him. 'In fact, the truth is, it has all made me very arrogant. No, actually, that's not true. I've always been very arrogant. I have become embittered. But I still have a lot of time for the old traditions of cricket. Play up and play the game – that is the only way to play cricket. I've got no time for the kind of cricket that is born in fear.'

I have never subscribed to the 'snooker is for wimps' theory, that the game is not a proper sport. Mentally, it is one of the toughest games around. Here is the I-hate-Steve-Davis piece: he won, but I wrote about the loser. Partisanship is one of the pleasures of sport: why should I deny myself such a pleasure, just because I am a writer?

NIGHT THE WORLD LEARNT THAT TO LOSE WAS TO WIN GLORY
May 1984

This was to be the occasion when snooker got found out. The world professional championship, sponsored by Embassy, at the Crucible Theatre in Sheffield was all set to be the event at which we realised how ordinary a game snooker is, at which the public, sickened by excess, at last turned away from this television plaything, unable to face the ghastly 17-day gourmandising banquet of unending click, clack, click, clack.

Alex Higgins went out early. The game was cheapened by awful Tony Knowles and his insufferable boasting about women. Boring old Steve Davis would win easily. Snooker had plainly gone over the top. In fact, I almost did not go up to Sheffield on Monday. Steve Davis was leading 12-4 over-night in the best-of-35 frames final, and it was certain to be all over by tea-time. Boring indeed. However, the man of the championship, the man who rescued snooker from cheapness and from any possible taint of predictability, still had a few surprises left.

Jimmy White, in his stand-up collar and made-up black bow-tie, face shining with the pallor of a man who never sees the sun, a man with the air of the second underfootman given to taking crafty swigs from the Madeira bottle, put on a truly, indeed almost literally heart-stopping performance, to make Monday one of the finest days of sport I have seen all year. He came back, and back, and back, until he was a single frame in arrears, the score 17-16 – the first to 18 taking the match.

Well, Davis won it in what he called 'the hardest battle of my life.' The difference between the styles of the two men is enormous. Davis seems never to have a difficult shot to play, because all the hard work has been done the shot before. White seems never to have an easy shot, yet he incorporates the impossible pot, the wildest long shots on which most people, Davis included, would play for safety, as a routine part of every break.

'You play a safety shot, and then he pots something from it. Does *wonders* for your game, that does,' Davis said. But on Sunday, Davis looked unstoppable, as inexorable as death. As a player, he is like an Alsatian dog: perfectly amiable so long as you don't let him know you are afraid. Then he is likely to spring at the jugular. With a nasty knowing air, he forced White on the run. Bullied him into errors, and gained a total psychological ascendancy. But White was still mentally absorbed in his thunderous semi-final with Kirk Stevens, that toe-to-toe slugfest fought out with utter recklessness by snooker's two young bulls. 'I wasn't even here on Sunday,' White said.

After providing such stirring sport with Stevens it would have been sad to watch him depart with a whimper, as he sat so helpless in his chair on Sunday, the insides of his cheeks practically touching as he drew life from yet another cigarette. But he came back enormously, opening Monday's first session with a break of 119, setting up the great battle betwen poet and engineer, between impetuousness and tactical acumen.

I have long loathed boxing. Here is the piece with which I came out of the closet on the subject. I find it hard to believe that there are people who consider boxing a sport. I have stuck my own head above the parapet on this topic on a number of occasions, and have been reviled for my inability to take a manly pleasure in the sight of someone getting beaten up. I will continue to write against boxing until it is made illegal.

THE IGNOBLE AND COCK-EYED ART OF SCRAMBLING THE HUMAN BRAIN
December 1984

You will recall the 'Thrilla in Manila.' I missed that. But I did manage to catch another exhibition of combat skills a few miles outside Manila a few years after that renowned boxing bout. I saw a fair amount of blood spilt. True, the crowd yelled in their frenzies, but their cry was for victory, for joy in the spectacle of combat.

It has to be admitted that some of the contestants died in the course of entertaining the crowds. Well, getting on for 50 per cent of them. And a lot of winners would never fight again, though there were a couple of fat, jolly chaps with needles and threads swigging San Miguel out of the bottle ready to patch up the superficially wounded. A good time was had by all, a lot of money changed hands, and everyone there, apart from the dead contestants, agreed that it was a fine day's sport.

The sport was cock-fighting. The sport is banned in Britain because it is a barbarous anachronism. The idea of training animals to injure and kill each other in order to provide a brief moment of elation along with the winning leg on a yankee bet is abhorrent to most of us.

And yet boxing, which in its essentials is cock-fighting with behemoths instead of birds, with gloves instead of razors, with wealthy businessmen behind the contestants instead of jeepney drivers with a ramshackle cock-loft, with the human brain the target rather than avian viscera, still continues. And just as cock-fighting does not demean the cocks, but the audience and the bird's connections, so boxing does not demean boxers, but the boxers' supporters and manipulators.

The British Medical Association has thrown its weight behind the call for the sport's abolition, and that meant that I paid a queasy visit to Harley Street listening to a neurologist saying horrible things like: 'The brain is the texture of lightly cooked scrambled eggs suspended inside a boney thing called the skull.' Dr Peter Harvey is a consultant neurologist at the Royal Free Hospital. A neurologist is a physician who deals with the physical disorders of the brain. And as you would expect, Dr Harvey has a particular reverence for this scrambled egg stuff. So much so that he has firmly thrust his head above the parapet on the issue of boxing.

'It is the nature of the brain that separates man from the lower animals. Boxing seeks to return us to the level of lower animals. People don't acknowledge that the *aim* of boxing is to cause brain damage. People point out that rugby is dangerous, that National Hunt racing is dangerous. They are perfectly right. But the aim of these sports is not to cause injury. In boxing, the ultimate achievement is to knock somebody out. And to knock somebody out is to injure their brain.'

Every year, we read about some poor boxer or other who collapses and dies after a boxing bout, perhaps as the result of a single, crushing blow. That is but part of the problem. Repeatedly being punched in the head has a subtle and cumulative effect. It has been proved that this has happened to boxers in the past: cases in the United States are still occurring. In Britain reports are more sparse, but again, still occurring. Twenty years after competition the ex-boxer can be found with slurred speech, unsteady legs, lapses of memory, violent tendencies, and the general appearance of having had a few too many. That is a chronic condition: the condition called, almost frivolously, punch-drunkenness. Or as the BMA report on boxing reports, in its sober way: 'Boxing is a contest in which the winner seems often to be the one who produces more brain damage on his opponent than he himself sustains.'

Dr Harvey decided to take up the cudgels against boxing, after meeting an amateur boxer twice, the second time a long while after the first. The physical and social decline in the man was immense: 'He had become a near criminal, a tragic man. The brain-damaged boxer becomes a social responsibility and a menace. Often violent, often a drunkard.' Dr Harvey fears that boxers are still unaware of the nature of the risks they take by boxing. But there is something of a communications problem between boxing and medicine.

The BMA report on boxing could only conclude by regretting that 'the British Boxing Board of Control appeared unwilling to co-operate.' Perhaps the organisation is uninterested in a boxer's safety. The Board refused to supply information, or even to send representatives to the working party.

Boxing has been made safer, not safe. Shorter bouts, less frequent contests, fewer mismatches reduce the problems: they do not remove them. As for the head guards seen at the Olympic Games: these make the head a bigger target and increase the torsional effect on the brain of a glancing blow. 'No, there is only one way to make boxing safe, and that is to take the head out of the target area. That would still give you a spectacle of unquestionable athletic skill. But when approached with the idea, boxing people are forced to admit that to take the head out of the target area would be to take half the fun away.'

There is a tendency for people whose sympathies are directed towards sport to hum and haw on the boxing issue. To mention notions like a government health warning on boxing, to say that people are free to have their heads beaten in if they wish. Dr Harvey is a neurologist, not a sportsman, and so to him the issue is refreshingly, brutally clear: 'The sport should be banned outright. It is kept alive by those who have a vested interest.'

It took Muhammad Ali to sum the matter up. He was asked in a television interview before one of his world title bouts, what he thought about the notion that boxing causes brain damage. He gave his sweetest smile: 'Who cares about the brains of a couple of black men?' Who cares about the brains of a couple of poor kids from any of the meaner streets of the world, for that matter?

However, in time, people will look at clips of boxing bouts like, say, the 'Thrilla in Manila', and be shocked that such barbarity was permitted by civilised people. Sooner or later, people will be appalled by boxing as they would be were the Albert Hall turned into a cockpit. The pity is that this change will come later rather than sooner.

From the Diary

No, said the boys of Ampthill Rugby Club. Definitely not. They are refusing to play against one member of Oxford Old Boys. The problem was that the player is definitely not a chap. Jean McCollister was – and is – a girl. 'I just happen to like rugby, and I'm fed up with all this nonsense about swerves and curves,' said Jean, who is five foot nine and weighs 10 stone. 'There are many men on the rugby field who are not as fit as me, or as tall.' The secretary of the club said he had checked up the rule book before selecting her. 'Nowhere does it say females cannot play,' he said.

That Steve Davis/Jimmy White match haunted me all that year. Why did I prefer White in defeat to Davis in glory? Is winning not what matters in sport?

THE CAVALIER SPIRIT THAT MAKES
FAILURE A GLORIOUS OCCASION
December 1984

Let's hear it for failure. And in order to celebrate failure properly let us go back to the Civil War. The most important result of this confrontation was nothing to do with constitutions, monarchy, parliament, religion or daily life. It was to provide us with a perfect pair of contrasting archetypes. All human beings in the world can be divided into two types: Roundheads, Right but Repulsive, and Cavaliers, Wrong but Wromantic.

Now, it is just possible that the alert reader might suspect that this is something of an oversimplification. What such a reader must do is to note that I am writing on the sports pages, those pages where the notion of excessive simplification as impossible. Sport deals only in excessive simplicities. True, you may find everywhere examples of subtlety of execution: a leg-side stumping, a free kick round the wall, a forehand down the line, a deep screw shot. But there can never be subtlety of achievement. You win, or you don't win: such a matter cannot be oversimplified.

Therefore, sports people tend to conform, in a rough and ready way, to the great, simple archetypes of the Civil War. Sportsmen are either Cavaliers or Roundheads. Cricket teams sometimes call themselves The Cavaliers. I never yet heard of one called The Roundheads, though perhaps there is one. If so, I expect Geoffrey Boycott controls it. He is the ultimate cricketing, indeed, the ultimate sporting Roundhead, dedicated to the mechanics of perfection. The qualities of the Roundhead are remorselessness, intransigence, inevitability. Though even Boycott has a streak within him, ruthlessly suppressed, of the Cavalier: witness his former tendency to impulsive hooking, his overexcitement at his hundreds – and no one who bowls with his cap on can be utterly without a certain Cavalier liking for nonsense.

If everyone had their rights, Roundheads and Cavaliers would be distinguishable at a glance. You only had to look at George Best to realise that he was a Cavalier, one of the finest examples there has ever been: delightful and doomed. Whereas the man who used to mark him (whenever he got close enough) at Chelsea, Ron 'Chopper' Harris, was nothing if not a Roundhead. It was not merely that Harris was bullet-headed: he looked as if he actually had a Roundhead helmet on his head when he was bare-headed.[1]

But things are not always so simple. Take Bjorn Borg: a Roundhead in Cavalier's clothing. For all his flowing hair, he was a purveyor of remorselessness. It was his unflinching competence, rather than flashing genius, that remains his enduring memory. McEnroe looks far more like a proper Roundhead, but he is really a Cavalier, a genuine purveyor of intuitive brilliance. A Cavalier who skipped his lessons in courtliness.

Head-to-head battles between Roundheads and Cavaliers are a regular delight. One of the finest day's sport in the year was the snooker final between Steve Davis and Jimmy White. White, hopelessly eight frames adrift, went raving mad, 'played his brains out', as Davis said, chasing impossible pots and impossible dreams, failing at the last but failing more gloriously than any winner ever succeeds.

Football is so full of Cavaliers that they have even invented a special term for them: luxury players. Players able to trap a ball and kick it beautifully are luxuries. Footballers able to trap a luxury player and kick him beautifully are the salt of the earth: proper, manly, non-pansified footballers. Room for both in the game, they always say, room for both in the same team, with Glenn Hoddle, the most luxurious player around, in the same team as Graham 'Referees seem to have it in for me' Roberts, who is perhaps the world's least luxurious footballer.

But it seems to me that it is the Cavaliers who tend to suffer in team sports. Selectors prefer competence[2] to excellence, probably because it is a commodity with which they can identify. If evidence were needed, then witness the international career of Derek Randall, a man who can be relied on in a crisis but not a cocktail party.

When excellence is sighted, it is disquieting. It is humbling. It is a quality remote from the spectator; hence the wish is to destroy it, to seek out the excellent man's demeaning qualities. Chase-and-harry footballers are not expected to curl 40-yard passes: luxury players are criticised because they do not chase and harry. Four doughty twenties is preferred to three ducks and a ton. And, of course, the Cavaliers always seem to play up to their critics, failing in the most embarrassing moments for their supporters and blazing away like men possessed – for they are men possessed – when even I have given up on them.

Ah, Headingley, Headingley, I hear you sigh, ah, Headingley in 1981, when the ridiculous Ian Botham, the Cavalier's Cavalier, performed a veritable Prince Rupert of an innings. So great an innings that, like Kennedy's assassination, we can all remember where we were when we heard of it. I was on a ferry in the South China Sea, reading the *South China Morning Post*. I hurled the paper into the air in inexpressible delight.[3] Botham even looked the perfect Cavalier then: it is my belief that he is half the player without his beard.

Of course, people will tell me that competence, remorselessness, and gritty, grinding inevitability are a part of all games, and so they are. But give me fallibility. Indeed, give me failure. Give me failure illuminated with shafts of yet more exasperating brilliance. Give me a single jewel in the wreckage of disaster. Give me the wrong-handed tip-over, not the comfortable catch; the lofted drive, not the nudge round the corner. Give me glory. Victory is cheap in comparison. Let's hear it for failure.

[1] This, I presume, is a joke.
[2] I think mediocrity was the word I was looking for here.
[3] I wish I'd had a quid for every time I have told this story.

From the Diary

Geoff Boycott now appears in a new avatar – as chairman of Melchester Rovers, the fictional football club led by Roy of the Rovers since 1954 in *Tiger* comic, and now in *Roy of the*

Rovers magazine. But how much does canny old Boycott get in director's fees? 'Nothing,' said the magazine's editor, Ian Vosper. 'Roy can't afford it. But Geoff's always been a fan of Melchester, he's met Roy, and said if he's not chairman of Yorkshire, he might as well be chairman of Melchester Rovers.' Boycott has been a writer for *Tiger* in the past, Vosper says, writing his own copy and even sending postcards to *Tiger* from abroad. It comes as a shock to discover that Boycott has a whimsical side.

> The Tewin Irregulars loom large in my personal myth. There are two ways of regarding a piece such as this: either self-indulgent to a degree, or a personal piece with universal application. I incline to the former view.

WARM MEMORIES OF BATTLES WITH TEWIN IRREGULARS
December 1984

This is the time of year at which sportswriters summon up remembrance of things past, and write about their fondest memories of a year's sport. I have no hesitation in nominating my own most cherished sporting memory of 1984. It was a brilliant leg-side stumping. The wicket-keeper was standing up to a left-arm bowler against a batsman who tended to play on the walk. The batsman was beaten by the flight, lifted his back foot for a fraction of a second, and in that infinitesimal fragment of time the wicket-keeper took the ball and, in the same superb movement, sent a single ball cartwheeling skywards. It was an unforgettable moment. I know. I was that wicket-keeper.

For me, the outstanding moments of the sporting year took place not at Lord's nor Wembley, nor Ascot, nor Wimbledon, nor Los Angeles. They occurred on the playing fields of Tewin, a village in Hertfordshire that has rather a good cricket team. I play not for Tewin, but for the Tewin Irregulars. The Irregulars were formed at the beginning of the year, born from a single factor shared by three men: uselessness at cricket.

Uselessness combined with a desperate desire to be better – or at least to play. What team would ever give a game to Roob, Salts and me? No captain is ever that desperate. Not more than once a season, anyway. But then we recalled our youth, and the games of pick-up football in the playground. There is always some fat kid who is both captain and centre-forward, regardless of his lack of any ability. But, of course, it is his ball. Now we reasoned, if we bought a dozen or so cricket balls Roob could exhibit his brilliant variation of length (he alternates double bouncers and head-high beamers), Salts could swish away outside the off-stump and I could buy a pair of enormous gauntlets and dive about. What greater happiness could be imagined?

Now I would not like to give the impression that we were messing about. No, indeed. We tried like mad in every game – dammit, we even won some of them. That was because we enticed some splendid cricketers to play for us, bowlers worthy of a better wicket-keeper, batsmen who played proper shots (one of whom even had different trousers for batting and fielding), cricketers who actually liked playing for us.

Our opening bowlers were swift enough to turn several competent batsmen and one incompetent wicket-keeper sheet white: who could fail to be amazed when the indomitable Fish fired them in like a bazooka off a leg-spinner's run? Murray, a Yorkshireman, at the other end, was the renowned purveyor of the 'plimsoll ball'. 'Aye, I like it when they come to the wicket in plimsolls. I bowl fast yorkers at their feet.'

One of the charms of an irregular side is the shifting nature of your colleagues. We fought out one nail-biting match with the help of a trio of quinquagenarian Cotswoldians with the wondrous Arthur taking three wickets with his sleepy-looking in-dippers. On another occasion we had four Indians, including a fearsome Sikh called Harinder. Had he worn his turban, I am sure we would not have lost, as we did, by a single run.

Garnering opposition was never a problem. England has hundreds of informal teams. The Victoria and Albert Museum beat us narrowly and were only saved from a hammering in the return by rain. Nelson Publishers were whacked. Grub Street Casuals made us field for three hours on the hottest day in the year, but still failed to win, tee hee.

It was a wonderful summer of cricket. Who can forget Roob's beamer at the opposition's coach driver, Murray's assault on the men of BBC Children's Programmes, Fish scoring 75 as a makeshift opener, the catches that clanged out of my gloves? The cricket varied wildly. With Murray and The Fish in full cry, fielders standing like greyhounds in the slips, wicket-keeper in terror of muffing a chance, the game is enthralling. Truly, this is the best of games, and we of the Irregulars try our best to play it in the best possible fashion: trying like anything to win and whingeing if we lose. Then having a pint.

Sometimes, we have two pints. In the company of the opposition (apart from once) and in full content. Never mind the grass stains all over your whites, or that the name of the maker of the ball is imprinted on your chest, or that the lying, deceitful batsman refused to walk when I had him, or the technical chance (as all dropped catches are called) that went to ground: never mind, it was cricket, lovely cricket, and if Goodwin got the yips and O'H got out for four, so be it.

The sun goes down, the beer is liquid loveliness in the glass, and though the memories and the trousers were then green, the trousers are now off-white once again, and as for the memories – as I write, already they are tinged with gold.

PART 3

THE TIMES 1985

Writing this three-part series changed my thinking about athletes, and about sport. I had been too used to seeing the stars as comic strip heroes, and their lives as thoroughly enviable. This was a serious failing of the imagination. The life of a professional athlete is one of daunting insecurity. It is not their physical attributes, but their abilities to cope with this life of insecurity, that makes the champions such remarkable people. Talking to the top performers about their insecurities opened my eyes.

THE YIPS: ANATOMY OF SPORTING MELANCHOLY
February 1985

In Japan, there is a class known as 'the window people.' The window people are fully employed failures. They have been left behind in the race for corporate honours, yet they remain embalmed on the payroll, with a job for life and nothing whatever to do. And so, all day long, in office hours, they do nothing but look out of the window. They are failures – but they are indistinguishable from everyone else.

There are no window people in sport. The *point* of sport is that everything is quantifiable. Success or failure can be assessed at a glance. There is no grey area. As the American football coach said: 'There ain't no room on the scoreboard for "I tried." ' Failure in sport is an appallingly public business. In order for sport to provide outrageous celebrations of might and success the way must be opened for the most abject public humiliation of the losers. Fear of failure is the most basic fact of life for everyone who has ever attempted to compete before an audience.

Golfers talk about the 'yips', the dreaded muscular twitch that affects a man who must sink a 12-inch putt to win – and who knows he is about to jerk it six inches wide. Snooker players get the 'snatches' when the all-important cue action disintegrates on a crucial shot. Tennis players suffer from 'the elbow', a nervous stiffening of the playing arm which makes for an instant loss of touch and accuracy. Darts players get a painfully comic failing called 'the sticks', in which they become so tense they are unable to release the dart, which ends up flopping humiliatingly to the floor.[1]

It happens in just about every sport. Sprinters relentlessly false start, footballers who can spray 40-yard passes with perfect accuracy miskick like tyroes when the target is goal. Cricketers get into all sorts of tangles, whether batsmen or bowlers. No sport is immune, because no sportsman[2] is immune to fear. The combination of overanxiety for success and creeping fear of failure can cause the skills that have been practised for a lifetime to fly out of the window. Let us, for the sake of convenience, refer to all such manifestations of fear as 'the yips.' It is a pleasing, almost an onomatopoeic term.

So, let us move to a couple of the more recent cases. Phil Edmonds, the England left-arm spinner, went to India and discovered that, inexplicably, he could no longer run up to the bowling crease. The stately graceful run-up he had used throughout his career suddenly deserted him at 33. He is reduced to a pathetic two-stride shuffle, from which he bowls quite beautifully. 'I had a similar thing happen to me once,' said Ray East, the Essex spin bowler and humorist. 'I had the stutters. I just couldn't start my run-up, so I used to do a sort of shuffle on the spot. I'd end up digging a great big hole.

'I remember watching Edmonds when he had another sort of problem: he just couldn't get the ball to pitch. He was sending some of them over the wicket-keeper's head, and our batsman was just helping himself. Well, Mike Brearley, his captain, kept him at it, and out of the blue, he produced the perfect ball, turning on a length and our man was gone, caught at slip. And then Edmonds went back to bowling rubbish. It was unbelievable.'[3]

Edmonds, however, was able to work through the problem before it overcame him. Another spinner, Fred Swarbrook, of Derbyshire, was not. 'Apparently he was bowling all right in the nets,' East said. 'But as soon as it came to a match, he couldn't get anything to land on the pitch. Everything was head high.' East, being a spinner, believes that such problems affect spinners more than other cricketers. Admittedly, it is the first principle of such bowlers that life is a complicated plot against spin bowlers, but there is no denying that the mechanics of the task are more complex than those required for bowling seam up. But no one will ever forget Derek Pringle's inability to get through a spell without an awe-inspiring collection of no-balls; a case of the yips, if ever there was one. Jonathan Agnew, bowling for England in Australia, has suffered from the no-balling problem of late, and said: 'It was becoming so bad, I was frightened to bowl. I was looking at the line, and not where I was going to bowl the ball.'

Then we have Mike Gatting, who had so many last chances as an England batsman it was scarcely credible. His low point occurred last summer when, twice in the same Test match, he was out leg-before without playing a stroke, arguably the most footling way of getting out in a game. It was a question of trying too hard, being desperate not to take silly risks. 'I don't get out like that in county matches,' he said. 'Everything is tuned higher in Test cricket, but that is not why I have failed. The failures were of my own making. You start to wonder if you should be playing at all ... and you should be doing *well*.' After 53 attempts he finally managed his first Test century, and there has been no holding him since. He was England's highest scorer in India. But then it was never his ability that was in question.

A 19th-century neurologist, Sir William Gowers, defined such occupational neuroses as 'a group of maladies in which certain symptoms are excited by the attempt to perform some often repeated muscular action, commonly one that is involved in the occupation of the sufferer. Other acts do not excite the symptoms, and are not interfered with. The most frequent symptom is spasm in the part, which disturbs or prevents the due performance of the intended action.' Jack Foster, a modern neurologist, has grouped together the occupational neuroses of writers, musicians, seamstresses, telegraphists, painters, money tellers, and even artificial flower-makers. But championship golfers could tell the whole bunch of them a thing or two about the yips.

Golfers tend to be admired, indeed, revered for their ability to hit the ball a long way. The finicky, piddling art of putting presents an extraordinary contrast in demands and techniques, and it can break the best of golfers. Ben Hogan had to leave the game because of his problems on the greens. Sam Snead adopted his extraordinary 'sidewinder' style of putting. Henry Longhurst gave up the game in disgust when croquet-style putting was outlawed – for it was only by putting in his way that he managed to beat his own case of the yips.

Golfers like to believe that the yips is a disease of the ageing player. But this is nonsense. The yips is nothing to do with muscular problems or with hand and eye co-ordination. It is to do with fear. And there are many players who find that fear of failure is something that grows with age. But Bernhard Langer was almost forced out of the game with the yips when he was a promising young man; so much so that in match-play golf, his opponents were asking him to hole every putt. 'You would have been stupid not to ask me,' he said. 'But it was awful, terrible to know that your opponents knew you would miss. And I did, again and again.'[4]

Tony Jacklin knows more about declining from greatness than any other golfer in the game. He traces the beginning of his slide from the very top to a moment when he was playing Lee Trevino for the Open championship, when Trevino played a wild chip shot that should have overshot the green but which fluked into the hole. 'On good days you don't hear the crowd,' Jacklin said. 'They shuffle and make noises, but they are part of your winning. But when you struggle, it's almost as if you're looking for someone to blame. Your hearing and sight are razor sharp, but in a different sort of way.'

It is forwards in football who are likely to suffer from the yips. The most notorious recent case has been that of Alan Brazil, who was deadly when at Ipswich but who failed at Spurs and is failing again at Manchester United. A former colleague at Spurs said: 'It is harder at a big club than at a team in the middle. We have to win all the time. The pressure affects some players, and it affected Alan Brazil. It was pressure, not lack of basic ability, that was the problem.'

It is not even skills or co-ordination that bring out the yips. Take the extraordinary case of Fernando Mamede, the Portuguese holder of the world 10,000 metres record. Every time he runs in a major championship race he either drops out or finishes well down the field. At the Olympics last summer he ran well in his heat, but in the final he was tailed off, and he ran, ran rather than walked, straight out through the tunnel in mid-race.

The yips is an extraordinary phenomenon ... and it can be a destroyer. For there can be no window people in sport. Peter Alliss, the golfer, writes from personal experience. 'Perhaps it is all a question of nerve. Perhaps one starts off in life with a supply of nerves, but simply uses it up. Unlike a car battery it is not rechargeable. So perhaps after all it gets back to the simple business of age, in the sense of having done so many years under pressure and having nothing left but the yips. Of one thing I am certain. Once you've got them, you've got them, and you will always have them.' This is a bleak and depressing view. And it is not true.

CURES FOR THE CRACKED AND FROZEN
February 1985

Barry Hearn, the snooker entrepreneur, manager of Steve Davis and others, and *capo* of the game's 'Romford mafia', has a theory about what makes snooker such popular television. Not only is every face like an old favourite from a soap opera, but you can watch them crack up before your eyes. 'There are

16 million people out there watching every twitch Steve makes. They say, look, I think he's cracking, look, he's beginning to go ... You are stripped naked out there on the table.'

Television snooker stars play brilliantly – and then miss shots most viewers would be able to sink. For such players, to miss such shots is like setting fire to money. This is trigger-freeze, the sporting phenomenon known as 'the yips', a golfing term used here to cover the intrusion of fear into the performance of every sport: a flinching from the moment of resolution which costs people their matches, their championships, their reputations, their careers. Many sportsmen simply never recover from the yips.

But some do. When Tessa Sanderson failed to qualify for the final of the javelin at the Moscow Olympics, where she was a hot favourite for a medal, everyone leapt to the conclusion that she was a 'choker', someone who dared not win when it really mattered. Whose technique failed, because her nerve failed. Of course, four years later, she won the javelin gold medal at the Olympics in Los Angeles. She defeated not only her own failure, but the expectations of the athletic world that she would fail again.

'In Moscow,' she said, 'it was my technique that went on the first and second throws. In the third, it was my mental state. I got so tight, so nervous. It was a shattering experience. I had been throwing the javelin so long that the qualifying distance, 60 metres, was easy. The Olympics is so much pressure, though. I thought I was coping with it at the time. But I wasn't. I got over it when I was invited to a meeting two weeks after the Olympics. I plucked up all my courage and went. I won, and I knew then I had not lost my ability. I knew I had not given my best at Moscow, that my best times were still to come. When I had accepted that, I was halfway to putting it right.

'In Los Angeles, all the papers were saying I would freeze again. Javelin is one of the most unpredictable events, but I was ready. I qualified with a 62-metre throw, rubbish, but what the hell, I was in the final. And in the final I had no fear. I didn't even notice a friend running in a race on the track,

50

during my final. Never has my mind been so strong.'

Bernhard Langer is one of the few men who have recovered from the classic golfer's yips – putting failure. Even now, this is a subject he does not care to talk about, but he traces the turning point to a victory in an under-25 competition. 'I couldn't stop laughing,' he said. 'Every time I hit a bad putt, the ball bounced off a footprint, or hit a spike-mark – and went in.' This from a man who once four-putted in competition. From three feet.

In rugby, it is the place-kickers who are most likely to suffer from the yips. Rob Andrew, the England place-kicker, had an attack when playing for his club on Saturday. It also happened to Mike Lynagh, a member of the Australian Grand Slam party. At one stage he began to miss everything, and lost his place in the side. Mark Ella, his colleague, said: 'His run-up was all wrong, his basic rhythm had gone. So he went back to basics, he just concentrated on hitting the ball sweetly, without worrying too much about direction. When you start trying too hard, your stride length will increase a little, and you find yourself too close to the ball, cramping your kick.' Lynagh solved his problem, and came back to score 21 points against Scotland, and to equal the Australian individual international scoring record. The yips can be defeated.

Steve Davis is always looked on as the snooker player who has the nerves of a burglar. But even the best of players in this most precise of games can begin to miss the easy ones. Davis is as methodical in combating the incipient yip, as he is in his break-building. 'I have a little black book,' he said. 'I have written all my faults in it. I check through it when I feel something has gone wrong. And in practice, I combat the faults by exaggerating the virtues. If I feel I am lifting my head in the shot, I will keep my head down in the shot for much longer than necessary. You must always be able to get back to square one. You must never get above yourself.'

Davis epitomises the method professional, rather than the inspirational have-at-you-now type. Is, then, the champion always the man with the least imagination? Not so, says Judy Simpson, née Livermore, the heptathlete. She managed to recover from a devastating attack of the yips at the world championships in Helsinki, when she was thrown out of the competition after three flat, non-counting throws in the javelin.

'Nerves can give you false starts, and can make you lose before you have even got to the stadium,' she said. 'You can lose your chance by imagining how things could go wrong. But that doesn't mean it is important to lack imagination. You must instead imagine how things can go right. It is called mental rehearsal, and it is a vital part of preparation. You imagine yourself in the arena, with all the shouting and the interruptions. Some people allow their imaginations to make them maudlin and moody. I used to be that kind of athlete, but I hope I am no longer. You must use your imagination to pull you up.'

Graham Gooch, the England batsman who yipped himself into a pair in his first Test match, talked about the tyranny of form. 'It is a double-edged sword,' he said. 'You play well because you have been playing well. Or you play badly because you keep getting out. It is a matter of working through the bad periods that come along.'

Working through it, having 'a belief in yourself' – these are the classic sportsman's answers to the problems of the yips. You are a prisoner of current form; only hard practice and patience will haul you to the end of the tunnel. It is very haphazard. The nascent industry of sports psychology believes that the whole business can be short-cut. The yips can be conquered through science. Nonsense? You ask Mark Falco of Tottenham Hotspur how he recovered from the dreaded goalscorer's yips, and he will tell you.

MIND GAMES THAT LET FALCO BEAT THE SCORING BLOCK
February 1985

There was only one thing wrong with Mark Falco's football, as his club, Tottenham Hotspur, pressed on with their challenge for the League championships.[5] He was winning the ball, laying it off, passing accurately, tackling back, and all that he was doing well. But he gets paid for being a forward. And he was not scoring goals. When faced with the goal, he would be inexplicably overcome with a total inability to hit a barn from the inside.

He was suffering from 'the yips', that mysterious loss of form that can affect all sportsmen and prevents them from fulfilling the most simple tasks of co-ordination, from performing skills they have taken for granted since childhood. Like kicking the ball straight. Ron Atkinson, the Manchester United manager, said: 'The skill level in the First Division is naturally higher than anywhere else in English football – but that doesn't stop players from having the same fears as those lower down.'

'There's not much difference between success and failure,' Falco said. 'But if you're on form, nothing can stop you. You get a bit of bad luck and things start to go wrong. It all started in a match when I hit the post twice and had another shot cleared off the line. After that, the chances seemed to come less and less. For some unknown reason, the goals started to dry up. I got to wondering when I would score again. I was doing everything right. But I couldn't score.' The Spurs manager, Peter Shreeve, kept Falco in the side. 'After he'd gone about 10 or 12 games without scoring, people were starting to give me sideways looks,' Shreeve said. 'But I thought if he was left out, the problem would get worse.'

Spurs employ a team of sports psychologists as consultants.[6] The organisation is called Sporting Bodymind. One's first reaction is that the entire field of 'sports psychology' is a load of half-baked nonsense produced by the jogging generation and the American worship of victory. A kind of made-up science. Such contempt, however, will not worry Falco because for him, the approach worked. His sessions with John Syer brought him back to form in front of goal: Falco has now scored 22 goals this season, one more than he managed all the previous term. Indeed, he scored Spurs' winner at West Bromwich Albion last Saturday.[7]

'John Syer came to me and said he could help,' Falco said. 'So I thought I'd give it a whirl. I'd do anything to better myself. One of the things he did was to ask me to remember how I feel when I score. To remember exactly how I felt, and to play it through to myself again and again. Never to let myself remember the misses, but to keep a library of positive videos of myself in my head.' When Syer talks about his technique, called 'mental rehearsal', he is particularly keen on the word 'kinaesthetic'. Mental rehearsal, he said, should not be a casual matter of self-indulgently flicking through the more pleasant memories of a sporting career. It should be seriously undertaken.

'I normally take two directions when dealing with a player who has a yips problem,' Syer said. 'The first would be analysis, a technical analysis in which I would get the player to break down what is going wrong, to make him be honest and realistic, and to work out for himself the best method of technical practice.

'The second direction is intuitive. I get a player to remember exactly what it was like, when he possessed the skill he has currently lost. Often when this happens, you will get a striking phrase. One player said that on his good days he was "like a pressure cooker with the steam coming out." Another said he felt like "lord of the manor". These phrases are a key to the feeling that has been lost. I might get the player to write the phrase down, and put it in his wallet, or on the notice board.

'Then with something like a scoring block, or a putting block, I get the player to stop worrying about the end, and concentrate on the means. To back off from the problem of putting the ball in the hole, and to concentrate on what he must do to achieve it. The person is helping himself. I question them, I make them be realistic. They are the ones who carry it out.'

The whole business seems, on the face of it, almost childishly simple. The skill is in the questioning, the understanding of the sporting mind and the problems it creates for itself. But the basic techniques used by sports psychologists are a rationalisation and an organisation of techniques that come naturally to any sportsman.

Anyone preparing to perform any sport will let his mind

dwell on it, no matter at what level he performs. On good days, indeed, this is one of sport's pleasures. One likes to look back at sweet catches, at great strikes on goal: a golfer likes to play over some of the most frightening or most inviting holes in his mind before a game, a horseman will jump every fence in his mind before he gets on his horse. Sports psychologists are using this natural function of the imagination as a deliberate training skill. Not just as a method of conquering the yips, but as a way to improve performance, and to sustain it. If mental blocks and fears can destroy performance, so mental tuning can enhance it.

In his book, *Sporting Body, Sporting Mind*, Syer skewers the phenomenon of the yips with uncommon neatness: 'All anxiety is accompanied by physical tension. When anxiety heightens beyond the point of positive arousal, the accompanying tension may be termed neurotic. Sometimes the tension comes from being stuck between the fight and flight response, part of you wanting to be there, and part not. Anxiety stimulates your flight response, but this is blocked by your wish to compete. This means you are using one set of responses to restrain another set, and the result is like treading on the accelerator and the brake at the same time.'

Falco said: 'I told John (Syer) that the first time I scored again, it would either be spectacular or a fluke. Well, it was spectacular. I've used it hundreds of times in mental rehearsal since. It was a diving header against Chelsea, from a near-post cross from John Chiedozie. The move fitted together like a jigsaw puzzle.'

The yips had been defeated. The phenomenon was shown to be not an act of God but simply a product of pressure and fear. A man-made problem and, as such, conquerable. There will still be sportsmen who get the yips, of course, and players who will be unable to conquer the disease, no matter how many sports psychologists they employ. But as sport becomes year by year more dizzyingly serious, and as training methods make ever greater demands, so it is inevitable that the training of the mind must play an increasing part. So that the athlete's body and the athlete's mind both become tools for him to manipulate at will. So that the mind becomes as much an instrument of the athlete's will as his body.

[1] Or they call it dartitis. Eric Bristow suffered from it a few years later, as mentioned on page 11 (note 2).

[2] I'm sorry, I should have used a non-sexist 'athlete' here.

[3] Edmonds virtually refused to talk about this when we worked on the book (see page 30). He just dismissed it as 'that time when I couldn't bowl a hoop downhill.'

[4] And it is a problem that keeps coming back.

[5] !

[6] This is no longer the case, though the organisation Sporting Bodymind works in many other sporting areas.

[7] That was very obliging of him; it gave a bit more street-cred to the entire series.

I have always liked David Gower. He bats like an angel on his good days, and this was written at the start of his great summer: when he took the Australians apart with the kind of insouciant savagery that is forever Gower in his pomp. He is good company, as well. He has been appallingly treated by the selectors, but then there is hardly an England cricketer of whom that cannot be said. Apart from Graham Gooch.

A WHEEL TURNING IN GOWER'S FAVOUR
June 1985

David Gower should have been a knight errant. Not only does he look the part to a quite absurd degree, but he also has a serious belief in the philosophy that sustained many a gallant in hard times, and which gave many more a sensible perspective after they had slain several giants and might otherwise be tempted to overdo the self-congratulation.

'It is the Wheel of Fortune,' quoth Sir David Goldmane, Knight of the Cherubic Countenance, as he mused on life, personal fortunes and the battle for the Ashes. As wandering knights were wont to consider the cases of princes who became paupers and beggars who became kings, rising and falling as the wheel turned ever on, so Gower can ruminate on fortune's frolicking with his own career as England's cricket captain. 'You are never convinced that your form has deserted you. You always believe it will come back. Things do build up, it gets harder every time, and it does get more and more difficult to believe that it will come right again. But it always does – it is the Wheel of Fortune, you see.'

But Gower had a depressingly long time at the bottom of the turning wheel with his knightly weapon losing its power, and the dragons simply not finding the middle of the blade. After two horribly public failures in the one-day internationals a few days ago, he was barracked by the crowd and condemned in many newspapers with suggestions bandied about that he would consider resigning as England captain.

That was the lowest point of the wheel's circle, and the climb back began at once with two successive centuries against Australia, one in a one-day international and the other for his county. It does one's heart good to see those magic little flick shots of his coming off again, the shots in which he stands perfectly still, moves his bat through an arc of 45 degrees and dispatches the ball like a bolt from a crossbow.

He is not one of those players who likes to go slumming for their runs. 'I *have* grafted for runs; been in a long time without making a lot, but my natural game is a little freer. But I tread a very fine line, my natural strength, and weakness, has always been my timing. If my timing is out, batting looks very hard indeed. At other times, timing is my best ally.

'People always talk about me not moving my feet. If you hit a four without moving your feet they say it is effortless. If you get out then it is a fault in your game. But the basis of my game has not changed, in times of good form and bad.' Gower's game is so delicately poised that there is no margin for error. A bread-and-butter nudge to point gives the pawkers and prodders of the world a certain amount of leeway. Gower specials give the batsman none: that is why watching Gower is either a great joy or a greater disappointment.

The theory is that it is the captaincy that has affected his form, the cares of leadership that have stolen his fluency, and filled him with doubts and fears. Gower does not give the classic sportsman's blanket denial of such a suggestion. 'I don't think the captaincy has affected my batting form – but I do think my batting form has affected my performances as captain. When I stood in for Bob Willis as captain in Pakistan, and made two big hundreds, the confidence I gained from batting helped me in the field as captain. If your personal contribution is a good one then your confidence is higher, you see things more clearly and you are more confident about the decisions you make. But poor form affects your decision-making.'

Good form and Pakistani glories were followed by the summer of the blackwash, last year's 5-0 defeat by the West Indies. Gower had a bad time and was not alone in that English cricket was crushed, and it seemed that the England captain was crushed with it. 'I felt by the last Test, when we were four down with one to go, rather like the character in the Spike Milligan poem – the one that goes:

The boy stood on the burning deck.
Twit.

'I think last summer's experience will get more and more galling as I get older. When the memories have faded a little the figures will still be absolutely clear. And I will wonder, when my playing days are over: 5-0. How could we possibly have lost 5-0?'

There cannot be many sporting jobs as demanding as England cricket captain. England football managers traditionally age fast in the job, but that is without the need to worry about their own playing performances. A cricket captain must answer to the nation for his team, his selection, his tactics, and his own form as well. Even in victory he has no time for celebration; he must go straight out to talk to the world's media, and when he gets back to the lads for a beer the lads have generally all gone home.

Sport is a soap opera and so it thrives on simple characterisations. Gower has acquired his own personal cliché, and clichés are always double-edged. A laid-back winner is a hero: a laid-back loser has been slacking on the job. 'I always play as if I had no problem,' Gower said. 'I am not a great one for scratching around.'

Doubtless, there will again be occasions when Gower is vilified for the fact that his laid-back feet are nailed to the floor; doubtless, there will be plenty more hymns for 'effortless' major innings of the future. 'It is a fickle game,' Gower said. But at the moment, as the summer's big matches begin, he is at exactly the right point of Fortune's Wheel and ascending nicely. At the beginning of the season, the simple assessment of Gower was that he was a struggling captain in a desperate hunt for form. By the end, he could be seen as the captain who, in successive series, won from one-down in India, and won the Ashes. Thus the Wheel goes full circle.[1]

[1] This piece is remarkable for the inclusion of a prediction that came true. Nor did the wheel stop there.

Remember the great Zola–Mary Decker hype? What fun that all was. To write about this in a critical or jocular spirit was certainly the shooting of a sitting duck. I gave it both barrels.

RACE THAT IS TRIPPING OVER ITS OWN FEET
July 1985

'It was the best bit of the whole Olympics,' said Eddy, pouring himself a White Shield in the Two Brewers. 'The Budd-Decker business, I mean. The two people I hate most in sport – and they fouled[1] it up together.' Even if you don't quite go along with Eddy here, you know what he means. There is something rather awful about both of them, and that little moment in Los Angeles was something of a crash made in heaven: the over made-up siren of the jogging generation,[2] with her all-American teeth, brought low by little Zola, the plaything of politicians and newspapermen, flying under her flag of convenience as Britain happily sets itself up as the Liberia of the athletics world.

I have always felt that Miss Decker – now Mrs Slaney since she married an absolutely enormous Brit – looks like a character in a soap opera. Now she is one. Yesterday she even referred to the ratings-topping Budd-Decker happenings as 'a saga'. 'There is something a little theatrical about it,' she added.

Mrs Slaney has just made her grand entrance into London; the crash made in heaven has become a match made with cheque books, and tomorrow we will have Son, or perhaps Daughter, of Los Angeles: the Budd-Decker re-match at Crystal Palace. Alan Pascoe, the promoter, described it as 'one of the big personality races of the century.' It all began to feel rather more like wrestling than athletics: Mary 'Toothsome' Decker against Zola 'Killer-feet' Budd – anyone want a ticket? Beamed live to the United States too; well, it would be, wouldn't it?

So there was Madame Slaney to face the cameras and the questions, looking large as life, and at least twice as natural, the big brown eyes of the world's sexiest athlete painstakingly outlined in black. 'So the business in Los Angeles is all forgiven and forgotten, Mary?' The lips curved minutely. 'I may forgive,' she said. 'I don't forget.' She has lost none of the ability that won her the title 'Whiner of the Year' in the United States.

Of course, the whole exercise is rather devalued by the absence of Maricica Puica, the Olympic champion, but at least her absence means that no one is going to get confused and start thinking that the event is mainly about sport. It is all about the fact that soap operas top the ratings. 'But the attention the event is getting can only be good for women's athletics,' she said. Hm.

Her race-plan is to go for a good time, perhaps as low as 8 min 25 sec for the 3,000 metres, to run from the front if no one else does, and 'to stay clear of certain feet'.[3] She added: 'I think Zola is a good athlete, but under tremendous pressure. In fact, if I was in charge of her training, I probably wouldn't allow her to run competitively at all this year. The pressure is detrimental. It can ruin you.'

After Mrs Slaney had made her glittering exit, and they had sent a man to mop up all the charm she had oozed, we had the surprise appearance of Miss Budd, looking rather nice, and wearing a blue woolly with a doggy on it. Even Eddy wouldn't hate her for herself. We have all read recently that Miss Budd has 'admitted' that the crash was all her fault. But the story, lifted from a television interview (done exclusively for an American station, naturally), was, she says, taken out of context. 'Both of us were to blame.' After the crash, with the boos echoing round the stadium, she says that she made the decision not to run for a medal. She didn't want to face the crowd from the rostrum, 'and I just didn't feel like running any more,' she said.

Miss Budd is not expected to win this race either. She has had a couple of recent defeats, in Belfast and Helsinki. 'I ran two bad races. I'm physically better prepared than ever before. I don't think I can win. Her times are a lot better than mine this year, there is an eight-second difference. But then, anything can happen in a race.'

She should know.

[1] A regrettable Bowdlerisation.
[2] I spent most of the following day being telephoned by American television stations who wanted me to say more horrid things about their darling Mary Decker in front of a camera. I told them all I was anxious to preserve my mystique.
[3] Bitch.

Fred Trueman has caused more radios to be drop-kicked through more French windows than any man in history. On a gorgeous day, one of the few times the sun came out all summer, I attempted to get a bit of own-back.

BOTHAM AND GOWER – HEROES AFTER THEIR TIME

August 1985

I do not understand. I just do not understand what is going on out there. The cricketers of today – they just do not belong on the same ground as the people of my time.

I remember the old days. I will tell you about one day, way, way back in 1985. England were 545 for three at tea – what times they were. We were playing for the Ashes, and let me tell you, in those days an Ashes series really was an Ashes series. It was at Edgbaston, on a Monday – I remember it like it was yesterday.

What cricketers we had in those days – not like today's shabby apologies for players. Let me tell you, standards have really taken a dive. But back in the old days, we had living legends playing for England – cricketers who never put a foot wrong throughout their entire career.

There was David Gower: what a captain he was. Never relaxed or lazy like today's players – he was just brilliant. Everyone gave unstinting praise to his timing – why, he never even needed to move his feet, not like today's lot. Tough and decisive in the field, hard working, grinding and determined as a batsman – that is the way we will always remember him.

I remember that day at Edgbaston, when he scored 197 before lunch, reached his 200 before we had finished our puddings, and we said then that we would never see his like again. And Lord knows, we have been proved right by the cricketers of today. Standards have slipped, I tell you. The Australian attack was the fastest in the history of the world, the leg-spinner was the trickiest ever seen, and as for the fielders, they did not drop a single catch all summer. But Gower was there and Gower was scoring runs.

And then there was Ian Botham. He was in the pavilion most of that far-off day, but I remember he scored 16 with his first four balls. What a man. How we all respected him. He was a bit of a lad, but no one ever thought any the worse for him for that. No one got the idea that he was bigger than the game, the way they do about the young fellows we have nowadays. But Botham was steeped in the finest traditions – he was a man of the old school if ever there was one.

Aye, that was the golden age of cricket all right. I remember 1985, when cricket was still a game for men. I remember it all. What a summer it was. Why, it was a summer blessed by the gods, when cricket was really cricket and the sun shone all day every day from April to September. Times have changed since then.

From the Diary

A man who has long umpired women's hockey is giving it up because he cannot stand the violence. Tony McGarva made his decision after a recent match in which a player pushed him in the chest with her stick after she had been ordered off. 'It was a very rough game,' McGarva said. 'Players were continually arguing and the language would have made a docker blush. I am too old to take this kind of aggro.' The North Humberside Ladies (!) Hockey League called for a full report on the game.

Glenn Hoddle is my kind of player. Here he talks eloquently about the way English football is suspicious of talent, hates the stuff. Getting Hoddle and me together to talk about the importance of flair over mere hard work was never likely to provoke a violent disagreement.

NATION'S GREAT CHANCE IS SPURNED
October 1985

English football's long love affair with mediocrity continues. The country's game has always displayed a touching willingness to accept second best, a vast love of the ordinary, a huge affinity with all forms of local self-interest and every one of the symptoms of terminal provincialism of the temperament.

So many people see the ludicrously gifted Glenn Hoddle as merely glitzy, as culpably inconsistent. They would prefer to see him fail: the concept is more their size.[1] In exactly the same way football's provincial self-interest has turned the World Cup into a minor competition. Hoddle said: 'The World Cup is the biggest thing in football. But as it is we are putting the biggest thing in football second to the domestic game.'

The Brussels disaster, and English football's consequent ejection from European competition, provided one of those unexpected pauses that give you a chance to reassess. English football's response to the challenge was to come up with the revolutionary notion that what the country needs is even more of the same thing as before. Given, for once, the time to think, football has decided that the way to the future lies in providing more and more and more of the stuff that the punters were already staying away from.

Hoddle is a player whose style exploits space and time better than most. He is appalled at the way that football has wasted the space and time created by the disaster. 'Every World Cup we say the same thing: England doesn't prepare properly. Then we are thrown out of Europe. The gaps in the programme gave us the ideal chance to prepare for the World Cup. The Mexican team have taken a whole year off from domestic football to prepare for the World Cup. But we shall be playing right through till May and then we will be chucked straight into the World Cup.'

The most telling response English football has made to the Brussels disaster has been to invent ever more spurious competitions. Presumably the idea is to drain the last drop of admission money from the hooligans before even they get catatonic with boredom. We have the farcical Full Members' Cup and the not-much-better Super Cup: motto, Who Cares, Wins. Football runneth over with cups.

'Instead of playing the Super Cup we should have got the international players together,' Hoddle said. 'The gaps in the programme provided the perfect opportunity to get the players working as a team throughout the season, playing matches and training together. But instead we have the current approach and it is amateurish.'

English football needs cheering up: even more, Englishmen who enjoy football need to be cheered up. To try to cure the depression with more and more depressing fixtures is obviously nonsense. Hoddle is right: 'All of English football desperately needs us to do well in the World Cup. If we do well the fans will be lifted and will start coming back to the clubs, more money will come into the game. If we won, it would turn English football around.'

It would, indeed. Hoddle, at last given something of a run in the national side, is more suited than most to the task of turning English football around. But the English belief remains: if a player is skilful it is taken as an infallible sign of something deeply wrong inside. English football is more at home with mediocrity. 'Everyone has flaws in his game,' Hoddle said. 'Because I have ability I get knocked for my defensive shortcomings. But players who are good defensively never get knocked for their creative flaws. In a team game you are trying to blend players: if I am 70 per cent creative and only 30 per cent defensive there are other players who are 70 per cent defensive.'

Football writers will write glowingly of, say, Platini, and then, in a hurt sort of way, criticise Hoddle for this inconsistency. 'Platini would get the same criticism if he played in England. Because if he played in the League he would be inconsistent. That's down to the number of games we play here: it is too damned hard for Continental players even to want to come here. What gives me satisfaction in football is to play in a certain way, a certain creative, artistic way. A First Division player will play 50 or 60 matches in a season: it is very difficult, perhaps impossible, to play every match in that way, to play as I want to play in every one of those matches.'

Hoddle believes that winning is important but that winning in the right kind of way is even more important: a concept too spacey for most footballing types to embrace. 'English sides like to play it fast and hectic. It is difficult for an artistic player to play in this system. But if an artistic player can do it in the English League he can do it anywhere in the world.' There is half a chance that Hoddle will be able to play at his best in Mexico. That is just as well. Half a chance is all he will get.

---

[1] Eddy (see page 59) is a great enthusiast of professional competence. He is an Arsenal supporter – well, he would be, wouldn't he? When he is most appalled at my own insistence on flair over and above less interesting virtues, he says: 'Let's face it, Simon. Spiritually, you're a *Tottenham* supporter.' He can think of no worse insult.

Here is another bearer of the banner of style: and as I learnt as we cruised around the Victoria and Albert Museum together, another crosser of the arties and hearties divide. But then, Jean-Pierre is not really all that frightfully English.

A BARBARIAN AT LARGE IN THE QUIET SPACES OF THE V AND A
November 1985

I love flair, style, individuality, unconventional brilliance. I loathe jingoism. Which means that in theory I must adore Jean-Pierre Rives. But throughout his career as French rugby's blond, blood-spattered hero, I have revelled in his failures and groaned at his successes.

Even when watching games like France v Scotland – to an

Englishman the approximate equivalent of Satan v Beelzebub – the mere presence of that spectacularly noticeable shag-haired villain was enough to get me shouting for the Scots. And when it came to Anglo-French encounters all the prejudices incurred by seeing *Henry V* at an impressionable age came swirling to the fore. I, sworn enemy of all who would reduce the game of rugby to a contest between kickers, found myself applauding the great boot as if it were the rugby players' long-bow, while I looked on the flowing French cavalry moves, inspired by the cavalier Rives, with utter disgust.

It is as well never to meet one's heroes. Reality is poor stuff compared with fancy. And by the same token it is wise not to meet those whom one has cast as enemies. They could well turn out to be insufficiently villainous and the disappointment is likely to be intense. I met Rives at the Victoria and Albert Museum. The deal was that if I could steer him round the 20th-century stuff, he would spare some time to talk. His enthusiasm was immense. 'Fantastique!' he said again and again. He has a soft spot for Art Deco, and fell head over heels in love with a glowing silver dressing table with pompoms on the drawers. 'Non, j'aime pas les pompoms.'

He is more involved in art than sport now. He retired from international rugby in 1984, after Scotland had robbed him and France (tee hee) of the Grand Slam. He still plays 'a little, just for fun,' for the Racing Club de France, and on such festival occasions as the Major Stanley match yesterday.

He now works for Pernod, which to an Englishman looks singularly appropriate. For whom else should so French a Frenchman work? He is involved in the establishment of a Pernod Foundation, which will discover, encourage and exhibit the work of artists. Rives is *un homme sérieux*. And the French have a seriousness about art that clashes with traditional English facetiousness. 'Isn't that hideous?' 'Non, you cannot say it is bad. You can only say, I do not like.'

Equally English, perhaps, is the reluctance to give things a go. Englishmen have a reluctance to be seen to do things they are not already good at. Certainly that tends to be true in the arts. One is a professional or nothing. Rives, however, is learning to sculpt: 'Yes, an amateur, of course, I do it just for fun,' but as fun goes it is naturally *sérieux*. He has had one work exhibited, which makes him very happy.

Rives also has that extremely French love of philosophical dispute. If you make a remark about the nature of life to an Englishman, he will tend to agree with you. Rives, being French, automatically disagrees: dispute is the preferred method of conversation.

'No, *everybody* expresses himself when he plays a sport. It is important for everybody to do so. To play sport is to express a part of yourself, your aggression. To play sport is to create. You must do a thing because you believe. If you are religious, you have *la foi*. If you are not religious, you must still have a belief in what you do. You must go out to create, to attack life.'

Rives played international rugby to win. But he could not help but impose his own passion for attack on any team he played for. His love of the open game made him a natural friend of the Barbarian tradition, and so became co-founder of the French Barbarians. I confess I had always thought this title was tautological before I met Rives at the V and A.[1]

He continued to lead a philosophical dispute as we retraced our steps from the Art Deco: his eyes were caught by a huge Buddha. 'They believe we have hundreds of lives. I wish they were right! But I believe that we have only one life and so we must – ah – go for it!' He laughed at his production of this piece of vernacular. 'It is not just what you do. What also matters is *le moyen*…. It is not what you do that counts. It is what you believe.'

I hope meeting enemies will always be as disappointing.

---

[1] This was maybe the fifth time I had used this joke, but it had been removed every time. I count its inclusion as a minor triumph.

I have completely forgotten the date on which this piece appeared in *The Times*. It was on the page opposite the letters and editorials – Op-Ed page, in jargon – in what had been at one stage the Miles Kington slot. The space no longer exists, in fact, which is a pity for me at least, because I have enjoyed lobbing the occasional piece into it.

TRUE – AND YOU CAN QUOTE ME

'What a marvellous quote,' someone said to me the other day. I was gratified: 'Yes, it was a wonderful thing for him to say. You can imagine how pleased I was when he came out with it.' There was a slight, and rather embarrassed, pause. 'You mean, he actually said it?'

Got it in one, I replied. I am writing pieces for a newspaper, not fragments of a Work In Progress. Every time I have said 'said', it is because the person said what I said he said. Or I said she said. It is only necessary to make things up if you are totally without imagination; people say interesting things all the time. All you have to do is listen, with your mind in gear. What people really say is usually more interesting and relevant than what they would have said, had they been a character in your novel.

But people find it impossible to believe that anyone quoted in newspapers has, in truth, spent all his life speaking in prose. When a surfer told me that riding a wave was 'like being one of those insects that mate once and die,' I was congratulated on my powers of invention. 'But he really said it!' Wise and cynical smiles were all my reward.

Reporters are doomed to be seen forever as myriad-minded men of the imagination, men with a huge appetite for inventing dialogue, men who knock Shakespeare into a cocked hat. For a reporter, it seems, an interview subject is no more than a glove puppet, a monologuing Sooty whose sweet cadences of speech stem entirely from the vibrant imaginings of the puppet-master.

The reporter could easily get carried away when he sees such a delightful image of himself in the world's eyes. But there is one certain way of restoring a sense of balance: try your hand at fiction. All of us seem to have lapses in that direction every now and then: the glory of winning the South China Morning Post Short Story Competition 1982 will be forever mine.

It is not *always* a mistake to write fiction, but it is invariably wrong to show it to one's friends. They know you make up every line of your newspaper reports; show them some genuine fiction and they come back with the following literary assessment: 'Paul is really you, isn't he, and Tamsin is that girl who became a Buddhist doctor, right? And Stephen is that bloke she married who you always hated, though that bit about you all getting drunk in the Chinese restaurant and then going tenpin bowling actually happened when you were with Chloe – that's it, isn't it?'

A work of fiction by someone you know has nothing to do with literature. It is a mixture of crossword puzzles and gossip; to a friend every *roman* has a *clef*. A friend's novel is not a piece of writing, it is a dead giveaway. 'I knew you were still carrying a torch for that Buddhist girl and her mantras.' Your toughly ironical conclusion impresses your friends only as an admission of eternal disappointment about events 10 years old. No one believes that a fiction writer is able to invent a single thing: everything he produces is forever seen as the most rigorous piece of documentary reporting ever produced. It is only when one turns to factual reporting that one's imaginative powers get any credit at all.

Did Proust have that trouble? Did his friends read his papéroles and say: 'Aha! Albertine is really your chauffeur, isn't she? And we've all worked out who Charlus is, but we daren't tell old Montesquieu…' On the whole, I expect he did. And I expect it infuriated him. Well, if he wanted credit for his imaginative powers, he should have been a sportswriter.

This is my hagiography of Ian Botham. It is a bit over-the-top, but if you bear both the date and the subject in mind, it becomes apparent that the piece could hardly be anything else. I do not repent of a single word of it. It was a grand summer, which ended with England triumphant, Australia crushed, and Our Boys leaving to fight the West Indies for the unofficial world championship of cricket.

BOTHAM'S BRIEF AND GLORIOUS MOMENT OF SHEER CELEBRATION

December 1985

This is the time of year when sports fiends argue even more than ever, indulge in even more rambling, pointless discussions than usual. It is not so much argument as an affirmation of a shared love of sport's simple-minded pleasures, a revelling in the unabashed childishness that sport is really all about.

And so as families gather at Christmas, the arguments begin: was Cowdrey better than Gower, what is a world team to beat Mars, Shergar was the best Derby winner since the war, there was never anyone to touch Best ... and, of course, the best discussion of the lot: what was the best sporting moment of the past year?

This is the best argument because all the top moments need to be retasted: Whiteside's Cup final goal, Torrance's tear-stained putting at The Belfry, Cauthen slipping the entire Derby field on Slip Anchor, Becker going berserk at Wimbledon, Taylor doing his nut at The Crucible, lovely Ginny Holgate at Burghley, Steve Cram's record spree ...

For me, there can only be one winner. It was a single innings by a batsman who scored 18 runs. It was 18 runs that exploded with all the joy that sport can bring a spectator: it was an innings of celebration – a celebration of the fact that we were about to win the Ashes, a celebration of the joys of sport, a celebration of the joys of living.

The batsman was I.T. Botham, the place Edgbaston, the occasion the fifth Test match between England and Australia. What a day it was![1] Robinson was out for a paltry 148, his feeblest Test century to date. Gower was at his most Gowerlike and played a glorious and glitzy innings of 215, Gatting played one of his fearfully butch innings and made 100 ... and Botham got 18.

Botham approves of bars and of conviviality. It must be a disappointment to him to know that whenever he comes out to bat, the bars around the ground empty as if the beer has suddenly lost its savour. And anyone who lingered to finish his pint that day missed the entire innings. For Botham decided to out-Botham himself. He acted like his own caricature. McDermott, the spearhead of the Australian attack, must have felt his heart crack within him as his first ball went sailing straight back over his head for a long, high, floating six. It was Botham's 100th six of the season, if you count one-day games – only his 75th if you do not.

The third ball went for another six, huge, meaty and glorious, that ridiculous club of his straight as a die. A few more runs here and there, and, after he had faced seven balls, Thomson caught him on the boundary and he departed with a ridiculous grin on his face. And the message was quite clear: We've won the Ashes, diggers. Hurray for everything.

Yet many people, I know, find Botham a deeply unsatisfactory figure. He is not a gent, nor is he a salt-of-the-earth pro. He is a show-off, a loudmouth, and he is always getting into scrapes. It was, in a ghastly way, almost endearing, and certainly inevitable that he should spoil his famous Long Walk by having that silly brush with the Cornish policeman. Indeed, one of his associates struck a bet that Both would not complete the walk without getting arrested. He was unlucky not to collect.

People tell me they get very tired of Botham, with his hair, and his air-thumping, and his Hollywood talk, and his brushes with the law, and all his over-the-top nature. But I say that he who is tired of Botham is tired of sport. Botham is a fantastic cricketer – and I pick my words with care. He plays cricket as if it were his solemn duty to live out the schoolboy fantasies of us all. His batting was scarcely required, save as decoration, this summer, but how typical of Botham that he can upstage an innings of 215 by scoring 18.

We had read once again that he was in decline as a bowler, and so he ended up the leading wicket-taker of the series, and the fastest bowler on either side as well. The man has made overachievement his daily bread, and in a decade or two we shall be talking nostalgically about the Botham Years.

Yet, while he is still with us, and still playing, he remains for so many people a *bête noire*. He has an unsurpassed ability to make people eat their words: after being criticised for dropping a catch at slip because he started with his hands on his knees, he proceeded to take a couple of absolute blinders – still starting hands-on-knees. The man is infuriating: and infuriatingly lucky, especially against Australia. Napoleon, wanted his marshalls to be, above all else, lucky.

The joy Botham takes in his cricket infects an entire ground: his delight in uprooting stumps, his revelling in his own power and might with the bat, his total love of being centre stage, make watching Botham on form the keenest pleasure in sport, and yet he remains the most tutted-over sportsman in the country.

I am not about to praise Botham for his off-field excesses, nor excuse them. I just love watching him play cricket. Anyone who does not can hardly, I think, love cricket. Yet people do resent his triumphs, do yearn for his pride to go before a fall, just as people willed George Best into his abyss of self-destruction and now talk with happy nostalgia about how we will never see his like again. I don't suppose we shall see the likes of Botham again. Anybody who says 'Thank God for that, then,' deserves to be barred for all occasions of sporting joy for life, since they obviously do not appreciate them.

[1] It was in fact the day already written about on page 62.

PART 4

THE TIMES 1986

The best way to write a column is to get the readers to write it. In the Diary one week, I asked innocently if there were any references to cricket in pre-cricket literature, flavoured this with the promised bribe of a *Times* fiver, and opened the floodgates.

CRICKET: FROM BIBLE TO BUNYAN
February 1986

Shakespeare was by far the finest cricket writer of them all. When I solicited hidden references to cricket in the literature of the ages, the response was startling. So many great writers have touched on cricket – even the Bible is filled with allusions, right from the moment when the Great Umpire started play and 'saw light, that it was good.' But Shakespeare is tops.

Many readers offered me that reference to the days when close catchers were slimmer than Botham and Gatting: 'I see you stand like greyhounds in the slips' (*Henry V*, III.i). Even more offered me a biblical example of poor spelling: 'And Peter went out with the eleven, and was bold,' which they all claimed was *Acts 2:14*. It isn't, in fact, not in the Authorised or the Revised Standard, but has achieved extraordinarily wide currency.

There is, however, a genuine Shakespearean precedent for

Peter May's speaking out against the reverse sweep: 'This is the bloodiest shame, the wildest savagery, the vilest stroke' (*King John*, IV.iii). And the bouncer is obviously no modern thing, but was in use centuries ago: 'You have broken his pate with your bowl' (*Cymbeline*, I.iv).

Nor is the turmoil that affects one of the northern counties a thing of recent years only: 'Alas, poor York, I should lament thy miserable state' (3 *Henry VI*, I.iv). However, southern traditions of gentility have long given rise to hostility from outsiders – hence the reference to 'the filth and scum of Kent' (2 *Henry VI*, IV.ii).

A Midsummer Night's Dream contains a clear reference to the last Ashes series, a remark doubtless uttered by an Australian perplexed with the wiles of Edmonds and Emburey: 'Hence, ye long-legged spinners, hence.' Interesting too, to note that the googly was known in Roman times: 'He put it by with the back of his hand, thus' (*Julius Caesar*, I.ii).

Antony and Cleopatra contains a nicely written – almost worthy of Cardus – description of Lillee appealing for leg-before. 'His legs bestrid the ocean, his rear'd arm crested the world, his voice was propertied as all the tuned spheres, and that to friends; but when he meant to quail and shake the orb, he was as rattling thunder' (V.ii).

It is hardly surprising to find the rumoured excesses of the England team in the dressing-room in New Zealand echoed in the Old Testament: 'Ben-hadad was drinking himself drunk in the pavilion' (*1 Samuel 2:9*). Evidence, too, that all cricket is morally reprehensible: 'He that touches the pitch shall be defiled by it' (*Ecclesiasticus 13:1*).

Weather played as big a part in cricket matches in biblical times as it does now: there is a reference in the Psalms to a couple of boundary fielders exhorting each other to get back to the pavilion: 'Deep called to deep at the noise of the water spouts' (*69:15*). Yet as every cricketer knows, rain can be a godsend: 'Thou, O God, sentest a gracious rain' (*Psalms 68:1*).

Then there is a mysterious reference to the sacred symbol of Anglo-Australian conflict: 'The priest shall put on his linen garment ... and take up the ashes ... and he shall put them beside the altar. And he shall put off his garments, and put on other garments, and carry forth the ashes without the camp unto a clean place' (*Leviticus 6:10-11*). The clean place the Lord's pavilion.

Dr Johnson was clearly a cricketer in Bothamesque mould: 'I never think I have hit it hard, unless it rebounds.' Elizabeth Barrett Browning, surprisingly, had a penchant for treating her copies of *Wisden* in a rather playful spirit: 'Do you see this square old yellow book? I toss i' the air and catch again.'

Bunyan knew a thing or two about cricket, and writes allegorically about the game: 'Then said Evangelist, pointing with his finger over a very wide field, Do you see yonder wicket? ... So I saw in my dream that the man began to run.'

A number of writers show an uncanny knack of predicting recent events. Shakespeare has it in *Pericles* that 'from ashes ancient Gower is come'; perhaps the man is older than he looks. In *Henry V* we have the undeniable, though unspectacularly expressed notion that 'Gower is a good captain, and in good knowledge', while Chaucer writes: 'O moral Gower! This book I direct at thee.'

The moral problems of the game have fascinated writers for several millennia. Omar Khayyam, in *The Rubaiyat*, tells us:

'the ball no question makes of ayes or noes,
But right or left as strikes, the player goes;
And he that toss'd thee down into the field,
He knows about it all – he knows, he knows!'

I would like to thank everyone who contributed to this marvellous mailbag full of great literature, and as promised, I will send fivers for every contribution here published. In the case of the many duplications, a single name has been drawn from the hat. I wish I had room – and fivers – to spare for the 200 or so other examples I was offered. These must be content with my thanks.

From the Diary

The British Medical Association is trying, but John Parris' wife is succeeding. For it was Mrs Parris who stopped the boxing match between her husband and Anthony Andrews in the battle for the Guyana bantamweight championship. Poor old Parris was getting a hammering from Andrews when his wife decided she had seen enough. She fought her way past her husband's handlers, grabbed a towel, threw it into the ring and clambered in afterwards in floods of tears to embrace her battered husband.

This piece is included for historical reasons. It provoked the most enormous row between Press and players. This was not because of what I wrote, but what was reported by Reuter's news agency, and printed in the local paper, the *Trinidad Express*. They took the strongest words that I had written, along with those of Ian Wooldridge and Pat Gibson writing for the *Mail* and *Express* and wrote a piece around them, on the lines of 'English Press criticise Ian Botham'.

OVER THERE AND OVER THE TOP
March 1986

Wouldn't it be nice if I was wrong? I'm so much an Ian Botham fan, you see. But it seems, from this Test match which, so far, has been a personal disaster for Botham, that the man has changed. He has changed from being an overreacher, an overachiever, into someone who is merely over-the-top.

His bowling with the new ball on the first day of the second Test was beyond belief. He strode out apparently to hijack the bowling, promptly set a field for the bad ball and bowled long hops. Not every opening bat is a junkie for the hook like the extraordinary Hilditch. Haynes and Greenidge rolled their wrists and smacked him all along the floor to the fence and they could have done so all day without giving a chance. In that first spell he bowled five overs for 39 which was 'a fair reflection of their worth,' as even the sober *Trinidad Guardian* said. His first nine overs cost 64, which would have been shaming in one-day cricket. Oh, 64 for no wicket, that is.

And his behaviour would have been shaming to a player in line for the man of the match award. He kicked the ball 30 yards in anger, he publicly harangued a player for conceding overthrows (wasting runs! – he's a fine one to talk, we all thought) and he yelled and made wild gestures at his captain when instructions to cut out the long hops caused him to bowl a half-volley, that was straight-driven for four.

His record on the tour so far has been dreadful – and yet his practice record has been worse. He has always been a lucky player, but one is reminded of the Gary Player dictum: 'And you know what? The harder I practise, the luckier I get.' Yet Botham seems not to have noticed. When Botham was a lad of 20 he could genuinely live it up all night, skive off practice and then go out and take a hatful of wickets. But he is an old fellow now, coming to the end of his career, and you cannot rely on strength and eye and inspiration at the age of 30. You need guile, you need intelligence.

Botham's batting has similarly been dreadful so far. He seems incapable of settling down at the crease: he seems only to think in terms of the cameo 20. That splendid 18 he scored in seven balls against Australia last summer was terrific and right in the context of that game: but that seems now to be his idea of the perfect innings. He doesn't look as if he expects to stay in long.

It is as if he believes all the hype and nonsense of his agent, Tim Hudson: as if he truly sees himself as 'a great British hero.' He struts on to the stage as a star, no longer as a professional sportsman. As if the scriptwriter had written in his sixes and his wickets and his air-punching celebrations, and all he has to do is look cool and go through the motions. Ah, he is such a marvellous man to watch, and it is desperate stuff to watch him act like a Mike Yarwood impersonation of himself, and to set such store by such things as the wickets of Patrick Patterson, as he creeps inch by statistical inch towards a new world record for Test match wickets.

When the last long hop has been caught on the square leg fence, and the record finally achieved, he will, perhaps, go on to Hollywood. But it seems that in his mind he is already there: negligent of team requirements and destructive on team spirit. Players commented on the difference between the spirit of the tour last winter in India[1] and this one – and they put it down to the long shadow of Botham. Botham acts like a star with a right to strut and bully and make an utter fool of himself [2] and he must take a healthy slice of the blame for the parlous state England are now in in this Test match. One hopes this matters to him.

Botham has a way of defying his critics and I would love to be defied today. But what real hope can one hold out for a struttingly self-conscious superstar with his head in Hollywood? Botham might go on to become a star of the silver screen. I can readily believe it. Indeed, right now, I can believe, if I might steal a line from the play *Pravda*, that Mickey Mouse wears an Ian Botham watch.

---

[1] Players always talk about 'happy tours'. A happy tour is a winning tour. End of story.

[2] This was the bit Reuter's quoted. The final sentence of this paragraph is terribly pompous, and is the only thing about the piece I have regrets about.

One of the pleasures of being a columnist is the freedom on occasions to go completely, savagely and irresponsibly over the top. What follows is an example of a writer hellbent on an attempt to outdo himself on over-the-topness and, I fear, largely succeeding.

ALAS, THE DARK AGE IS UPON US AGAIN
August 1986

August is the cruellest month, bringing football out of the green land, mixing memory and desire and making us all as sick as a parrot in the process. The ghastly, horrible Charity Shield, that harbinger of winter, is the most loathsome event in sport because it brings with it the return of football, cold days and misery. Few of us will have any charitable thoughts for football today: rather we will call down curses on the game from every direction.

Newspapers always greet the return of the football season with incomprehensible glee. 'Robson Out Seven Games,' declares one, inducing a vertiginous feeling of *déjà vu*. I am sure that some newspaper editors have made a religious vow to print the same picture of Robson rolling about in agony on alternate days throughout the football season. 'Robbo Crock Shock' is permanently set in type for use at least once a week. 'Spurs Stole Our Kid' ... 'Mick Channon Lifts The Lid Off Soccer' ... the sport's essential veniality is conveyed with almost pedantic care by some newspapers, and the sense of depression this brings with it, all-encompassing.

Footballing depression is an annual event, of course. That is inevitable. The start of the cricket season is a wholly different occasion, full of good cheer and optimism, for it is the herald of summer and of longer and warmer days. But football, intemperately rising in the middle of summer, reminds us only of winter: short days, chilled bones, and the battering the spirit takes during weeks on end without the sun. All the inherited miseries of primitive man who knew as the days shortened that his cave would become more hideous and his life harder with each night of the coming winter, are recalled in the return of the football season. A single mention of Ron Atkinson recalls countless aeons of suffering.

Every year, football steps rudely and unwelcomed back into our lives. It does so again this year, despite, or perhaps because of, the pleasures of the summer's World Cup. For we know the English season will not bring us the glorious follies of the Danes, the flair of the Soviets, the heart-lifting skills of the Brazilians and the French. We will get lots of running about instead. 'Come on son, pressure, pressure, pressure,' the coaches will yell: pressure, the substitute for skill, and one away point, the substitute for glory.

And when football comes, the morons are never far behind.

What fully sane person would go to a football match for pleasure? To travel in an unspeakable atmosphere of threat and watch a poor game played to the sounds of witless abuse: is this what Saturday afternoons are for? No wonder more and more people watch television.

England has greeted the first knockings of the football season with riots abroad and riots on the Channel: any European club that fixed a pre-season friendly with an English club must be run by lunatics. English football is desperate to return to European competition, but I don't think English clubs should ever be allowed back. True, the football in these competitions is often pretty good, but the price is far, far too high.

It is impossible for any football match involving an English club to take place without an enormous number of policemen. This is absurd. If public meetings ever gave rise to such predictable disorder, they would be banned from taking place. Perhaps the answer is for the law to make a pre-emptive strike against footballing disorder: anyone who agrees to play a football match against Chelsea should be charged with behaviour likely to cause a breach of the peace.

English football is followed by poisonous people, and Europe was quite right to get rid of them. The more they ban English football, the less trouble they will get from the canaille that comes with it. There is a lesson here for England. England should follow Europe's lead. English clubs are banned from European competition: they should now be banned from domestic competition as well. That will do the trick. That will certainly make the month of August less cruel.

The Somerset Crisis, which ended in the sacking of Viv Richards and Joel Garner and the resignation of Ian Botham, was the usual grubby political affair, with all kinds of nastiness thrown in. Despite my own high regard for flair over humdrum qualities, I found myself drawn to Peter Roebuck, and the essential right-minded sanity he always seems to represent. The nature of the story was not merely local: it was also about the nature of county cricket and the tensions that destroy teams.

EXPOSED: INNER RING OF SOMERSET CIRCUS
September 1986

There are two ways of looking at The Great Somerset Crisis. The first is that it is another of those nasty little squabbles that sporting organisations tend to go in for. The second is that it is a battle for souls: the soul of a cricket club and the soul of English county cricket.

County cricketers lead an extraordinary life. Anyone who has read Peter Roebuck's superb book *It Never Rains*, a season-long diary of a careworn batsman, understands something of the relentlessness of the seven-days-a-week season. 'Monday was a poor day. Charging about the country, trying to live up to a high level of expectation and performance, had been a burden. I wanted to disappear for a week, or for a month, and yet was expected to "keep buggering[1] on"... I wanted to be able to relax, to be sociable, to become more human – it's in there somewhere, but one has to suppress so much of it to win the battle. Then suddenly you realise the battle is not worth winning.'

But Roebuck is now the captain of Somerset, as well as being one of the best two cricket writers[2] in operation. Many see him as the man behind the Great Crisis: the decision not to renew the contracts of the overseas stars, Viv Richards and Joel Garner, which prompted (by design? people ask) Ian

Botham to announce that if his mates went, he went too. This is not exactly the case but Roebuck is clearly aligned with those in favour of the decision. If it is overturned at an extraordinary general meeting of the members in October Roebuck will have to go as captain and probably as player.[3]

At the core of the argument is the difference between the ordinary county player, the sort whose anxious life is made clear in Roebuck's book, and the star. But stars are greedily signed up by counties who want inspirational cricketers to perform deeds of magic seven days a week. Often they cannot find such inspiration, they cannot make themselves care enough. Some – Hadlee, Marshall, Daniel – are genuine through and through. Others get the reputation for being non-triers. They get injuries, they leave the field when it suits them, they keep missing matches. Funnily enough, the groin strain never strikes for one-day finals: but when there's a midweeker in Glamorgan, stars suddenly find themselves unable to lift a bat. The need to find success united Somerset, players and stars alike: the effort of sustaining it seems to have been utterly divisive.

The question is whether a county cricket club is a circus for the stars to perform miracles at one-day games when the crowds turn up, or whether it is about winning county championship games in front of a few dozing members. On dull days, and there are many, stars like to withdraw to the pav with a muscle tweak to let the duller virtues of duller players make themselves plain.

The star system can work for a county but it depends very much on the star. That is why Somerset have moved for Martin Crowe. On cloudy Wednesdays at Derby when even the dogs fail to show up they believe Crowe will get his head down and score runs. Other stars manifestly do not always find this motivation.

But the fault is not only with these other stars, it is also with the county championship itself. No other country plays such relentless cricket as England. The pros spend their lives roaring up and down motorways, jockeying in the outside lane in slightly underpowered sponsored cars, eager to get home. It is a wonder that cricketers do not all perish on the M1.

This is not a life that all superstars can learn to love and

Somerset are over-endowed with big occasion specialists. There is a gang, an Inner Ring of stars at Somerset: nothing more eroding of team spirit could be imagined. Indeed, a Botham Inner Ring has affected the England as well as the Somerset dressing-room: Botham loves gangs, he's that sort of fellow.

It is this that Somerset are trying to end with the proposed departure of Garner and Richards. They want good, solid cricketers trying hard, playing consistently, looking good in the county championship. It is the sort of thing members like. Occasional supporters could not care less, but it will be members that vote on the decision. Letters are flooding into the club and are 60-40 in favour of the stars' departure. Members love the county championship: stars often do not. There is so much of it: Phil Edmonds said he could go on for years if he were playing for England and Highgate. In his last few seasons Bob Willis was a lion for England and a lamb for Warwickshire. This attitude can provoke both the anger and the envy of the salt-of-the-earth pro.

The county championship is an incredible fag and it takes special and not always exciting virtues to do well in it. Tim Hudson, Botham's former agent, spoke out in favour of turning the county championship into a training ground for the under-25s and turning the rest of the game into a travelling circus of the stars. Hudson is wont to talk about such people as Richards and Botham as 'rock 'n' roll cricketers.' The Somerset battle is about whether cricket is about steadiness, loyalty, perhaps a little dullness and certainly a lot of genuineness – or about rock 'n' roll.

[1] One of the real achievements of the year was to get the word 'buggering' in the paper. Getting bad words in the paper is one of the puerile but enormous pleasures of any newspaperman. One of my most treasured lines in any review of one of my books was in *Wisden Cricket Monthly*, which said that 'even the obscenities were more or less justified.'
[2] I wonder who the other one was. Certainly this line was meant as a tease for various friends and acquaintances in the Press box. Either Matthew Engel of *The Guardian* or our own John Woodcock, I would guess from this distance.
[3] The Roebuck side won, of course. Roebuck stayed as captain until the end of the 1988 season.

From the Diary

Lord Byron's cricketing career has recently been recalled by the display of a letter at Harrow School. Byron played in the first Eton v Harrow match in 1805 (Eton won by an innings and two runs) and wrote afterwards: 'We have played the Eton and were most confoundedly beat, however it was some comfort to me that I got 11 notches in this 1st innings and 7 the 2d, which was more than any of our side except Brockman and Lord Ipswich could contrive to hit. After the match we dined extremely friendly, not a single discordant word was uttered by either party. To be sure, we were most of us rather drunk, and went together to the Haymarket Theatre where we kicked up a row, as you may suppose when so many Harrovians and Etonians meet at one place. We all got into the same box, the consequence was that such a devil of a noise arose that none of our neighbours could hear a word of the drama, at which, not being highly delighted, they began to quarrel with us, and we nearly came to a *battle royal*. How I got home God knows.'

Here is another sympathetic piece on David Gower. I do not say that he is the greatest captain of all time … only that he is the most successful captain since Mike Brearley. Perhaps, had he gone to South Africa with the Brewery rebels, he would have been treated more lovingly by the selectors.

GOWER THE RIGHT MAN
AT THE WRONG TIME
September 1986

David Gower lowered his world-weary lids, flicked an imaginary speck of dust from his irreproachable Mechlin lace cuff, and spoke of triumph and disaster in the same way: with a faint, fleeting smile and a self-deprecating ironical quip. Well, the bit about the cuff isn't literally true, but Gower is not so much a modern 'laid-back' character as a throw-back. He is the sort that greets triumph with 'that didn't go too badly' and disaster with 'it's only a scratch.' He will tell the world: 'It was nothing really.'

And so he is slightly out of kilter with his time. Cricket now gets an enormous, an unprecedented amount of national attention: the popular demand is for some rah-rah chest-beating PR man of a captain. The literal-minded tend to believe Gower when he says his achievements are but nothing, and when he faces defeat with another ironical quip, they think he is no better than frivolous. They forget the English tradition of facing the mightiest of circumstances with a light laugh. 'It was,' said Gower, 'the year of being seen to do things.'

This is effectively what Gower was told to do in the first Test of the summer. His response was to wear a T-shirt bearing the words: 'I'm in charge.' Not everybody liked the joke. England lost the match and Gower, the captain who won from 1-0 down in India and then won the Ashes, was sacked. His response was to give the T-shirt to his successor, Mike Gatting. I don't suppose it was a perfect fit. It has not shown itself to be yet.

'The T-shirt was, perhaps, a mistake,' Gower said. 'But I couldn't resist it. For captaincy means more than vigorous arm-waving. So much of it is hidden from spectators. So much is hidden from the chairman of selectors. The demotion hurt.' He then added, with one of the faint, fleeting smiles, and perhaps just the smallest hint of malice, 'Still, at least that saved me from having to explain two serious defeats.' An England captain has to do a lot of explaining these days. Football is in decline, and cricket – Test cricket – gets more public attention than ever before.

This is what the new era of cricket is all about. We have been used to headlines like 'The End of The World' when the football team gets knocked out of the World Cup, but now the same massive reaction to victories and defeats is part of cricket's pattern. The ironical quip is out of joint with such times. Gower's great fault is nothing to do with cricket: it is just that he has mismanaged his own PR.

After the Ashes win, England were expected to do all right on the tour of the West Indies. But the first Test, played on a snake-pit wicket at Sabina Park, Jamaica, was an unmitigated disaster. 'It took a lot of heart out. It almost destroyed the tour,' Gower said. The depth of the disappointment was shattering. 'I have been around in the past when things have gone wrong. But this time it was seen as a national disaster. Even when things went right, people thought there must be something wrong behind it.'

Sports critics have never properly understood Gower's enigmatic public persona. He was the man who greeted England's Ashes win by saying: 'The West Indies will be quaking in their boots.' It is simply that the traditional pose of the English hero, of assumed nonchalance under the pressure of both victory or defeat, suits Gower well. He would be uncomfortable making avid public statements. It is a comfortable mask for a deeply self-conscious man.

But what a year it has been: Gower has been sacked as England captain, removed as captain of Leicestershire, and now passed over as vice-captain for the tour to Australia. If the first two can be regarded as policy decisions, the third looks like an out-and-out snub: what is, it must be hoped, the last personal disaster in the worst year he can remember.

The year's troubles began with the death of his mother. Cricket watchers tend to discount such things. Such ordinary problems cannot, they feel, affect a semi-fictional character like a sporting star. But they do. Gower's last 10 days in England before the West Indies tour were spent clearing up his mother's house and arranging her funeral. Most people have to face such sad times: all are affected by them. Gower arrived in the West Indies quite exhausted. And let himself off the first match to recover. In retrospect, this was his first PR mistake. Then came the Sabina Park Test and the juggernaut of defeat was off and rolling. With the attention of the world on them as never before, the failings of the team were appallingly public.

Then came Gower's famous last words. Politicians know all about famous last words: the single line that destroys you forever. The pound in your pocket will not be worth any less, or prices will be cut at a stroke: that sort of thing. Gower's famous last words were: 'Voluntary net practice.' A howl of disbelief rose up at this; all cricket followers were suffering disappointments because of the result: they wanted to see those boys out there suffering too. Again the PR had gone wrong. 'The truth is, we flogged our guts out with preparation. All of us, especially at the start. But the tour wore everybody down. There was no point in calling an eight o'clock curfew, or taking all the beer out of the team room. And often, there weren't proper practice facilities anyway.' But 'voluntary nets' did for Gower all right.

Here is a quick quiz question: Who was England's top scorer in tests in that West Indies series? Answer: David Gower. Despite that, the first home Test of the new summer was Gower's official last chance. He lost, got fired, then got a shoulder injury and missed the next Test. He came back for the third, and played well. 'So people started to say I was better off without the captaincy. Then against New Zealand they said I was jaded. I scored 62 in the first innings and they did a 180-degree turn. I did badly in the second and they did another 180-degree turn. I was niggled. They said I should be rested for the next Test, and I could almost have gone along with them. But there's a danger in that: if you don't go out to meet the thing, you start to go backwards. It is hard to build yourself up again. So I stayed in.'

Second quiz question: Who was England's man of the series against New Zealand? Answer: David Gower. After that, he took the rest of the season off to recuperate. Well deserved, I should think, and certainly much needed.

He has also been replaced as Leicestershire captain. Next season is his benefit, which is the reason, or excuse, for the change. 'I would like to get the England captaincy back again, but it goes against all historical precedent. And it would mean wishing evil on Mike Gatting, and I couldn't do that. But I miss it: the motivation to play well is greater for a captain. You feel it must be you that gets the runs. No matter how you feel, you must dredge something up. That's important to me, being the sort of player I am – I know, for example, that I should have made hundreds. Hundreds that greedier players would have got. I've made too many nice 80s and got out.

'I wish I had been made vice-captain for Australia. I started as England captain very much as a novice, and after 16 months I had run the gamut, done the apprenticeship.'

Gower greeted his success as a captain with self-deprecation. Richie Benaud recommends captains to take all the praise they can when it is offered, because they'll certainly have to take all the blame when they lose. But Gower is not the man for extreme reaction. He is too intelligent, too much aware that things change, too much aware that sport is not the only thing in the universe, too much, in his soul, an amateur, a throw-back. Neither selectors, nor his public, seem to have truly understood that his flipness is no more than a comfortable pose. But this, after all, has been the year of being seen to do things.

I know I go on about boxing being a bad thing. There is a counter-argument I often get that says, what about steeplechasing then? What about motor racing? But I certainly don't object to danger in sport. Sports without a slice of danger in them lack something. Cricket, think some, is the most gentle of games, but it is not. That ball is bloody hard, and fast bowlers don't bowl quick just to defeat your co-ordination. They want you to be frightened. When you get hit, it hurts: that's what gives the game its zing. And so I compiled a five-part series on *really* dangerous sports.

JUMPING FOR JOY FROM A GREAT HEIGHT

September 1986

Sport is the ultimate trivial pursuit. Its triviality is rather its point. It just doesn't seem all that trivial at the time. In every game that was ever played, players have thought: 'I would die for the chance to score the winning goal/make the crucial catch/finish in front of the others.' But even as they think it, they know this is just a figure of speech. Their death isn't actually necessary.

But there are some sportspeople who really do face death every time they go out to play. They don't think about it quite like that, of course, and they certainly don't talk about it like that. But they all accept the fact that every time they go out to play they could come back dead. Climbing mirror-smooth cliffs, racing Formula One cars, setting waterspeed records, riding horses over fences at what are, literally, breakneck speeds: these are not sports for everyone. Most people love safety, love survival too much.

The sport that calls for the total defiance of all the survival instincts that have been acquired by man is parachuting. To climb is one thing: to fling oneself at the ground from a dizzy height is quite another. 'Bloody rock climbing, you wouldn't get me doing that. It's dangerous,' said Charles Shea-Simmonds, survivor of more than 2,000 parachute jumps. 'You have to rely on other people, too. In parachuting you are on your own. Right from the very first time you do it, you are alone. And that's awesome.'

Shea-Simmonds is one of the founding fathers of sport parachuting in Britain, and is vice-president of the British Parachute Association. Like anyone involved in any risk activity, the first thing he tries to do is to convince you how safe it all is. 'Two of my kids parachute, and I'd be a lot more frightened if they rode motorbikes.'

Insurance companies still speak to them, and the sport had a seven-year period without any deaths. This record has ended, however: in recent weeks there have been two civilian parachuting deaths, one in Shropshire, one in Lincolnshire; both have still to come up before the coroner.

A character in a Gavin Lyall thriller is asked about parachuting. 'I thought it was supposed to be very exhilarating, once the chute opens.' 'It is, if you think of the only alternative.' And everyone who does it enough, will, no matter how cool he is, have his share of moments that terrify him.

Shea-Simmonds was involved in one mass jump that missed multiple deaths by the kind of margin that would make the stubbornest sceptic in history turn to God. There were parachutists jumping from two planes, which were supposed to be flying alongside each other. But one slipped, undetected, below the other at the crucial moment: Shea-Simmonds jumped and missed the plane below by a coat of paint; the second man hit it and broke his leg; the third man dived head first through the roof.

Shea-Simmonds completed his jump and looked around him. He counted 11 of 14 jumpers, and believed then that three people were dead. But not so. Eventually, he saw a parachute high above. The second man had hit the plane and opened his chute at once and was in the middle of a 12,000-foot descent, one in which he spent every second thinking about how he was going to land on his broken leg. Another man, seeing the mayhem below, didn't jump. And the other man landed inside the plane he had holed. He had broken both wrists and was in terrible pain, but kept shouting to his helpers: 'For Christ's sake, don't cut my boots!' Expensive things, you see.

The man was Mike Bolton. The accident hardly put him off the sport: he has made more than 1,000 jumps since then. 'I remember seeing the plane below and throwing up my hands to protect my face,' he said. 'I hit the fuselage dead centre. If I had not, I would have bounced sideways into the props. When I close my eyes, I can still see the props. I came through the top of the plane, hit the one and only seat, which broke my fall, and landed half in, half out of the door. I wasn't sure whether to stay in or throw myself out, but I thought it best to stay. Afterwards, I never considered giving up. It was just that the next time I jumped with two planes I was, shall we say, a little slow on leaving.'

'Every time you step out of a plane it is a moment of truth,' Shea-Simmonds said. 'You know that if you do nothing, you are dead. You don't think of it like that, but you know it is true. And the thing is that you totally control the level of risk. I have had five malfunctions, and at least three of them have been my own fault.

'It is not frightening though, not exactly. It involves … ah … an acute sense of apprehension. Especially the first time. You have to get a grip. It's not like kicking a football about in a yard. You know, I always hated sport at school. But the first time I saw someone drop from 5,000 feet, I thought, my God, I've got to do that.'

For years he did little else: Parachute Regiment, British parachute team, founding his own parachute club. He runs a small specialist packaging firm, hates London, lives in Wiltshire. He has three children, two of whom have parachuted. 'The people who do it are a special breed. We all play down the risk element, but we all know that the sky is far more unforgiving than the sea ever is.' So, one imagines, is the ground. 'But it would be a sad society without people who take risks. A little apprehension does no one any harm.'

Fear is part of the point. You have to be frightened first, if you are going to conquer fear. But there is more to it than that. Sky divers have tried to explain, have adopted phrases from Richard Bach's highfaluting book of aerial mysticism, *Jonathan Livingstone Seagull*: 'Perfect speed is being there…. The gull who flies highest flies furthest….'

'I'm not a poet, I can't tell you how it feels,' Shea-Simmonds said. 'But I know that risk sharpens things up, makes you more aware. You have an increased perception of things…. You know…. how green the bloody grass is….' He gestured hopelessly. If you haven't been there, you can never quite understand, and if you have been there, you can never quite explain. 'But I don't parachute because I like the idea of dying. I parachute because I enjoy living so much.'

CHALLENGE OF SURVIVING IN CAMPBELL'S KINGDOM

September 1986

Donald Campbell spent most of his life flirting with death, yet when he died it shocked us all. I expect many people can remember where they were when they heard the news, it was that kind of event: how this apparently indestructible man, who always looked as if he had stepped elegantly from a wind-tunnel, was killed in pursuit of the world water-speed record, after his boat, Bluebird K7, aerodynamically designed like an aeroplane, flew from the water at close to 300 mph and crashed back murderously. At the time, in 1967, it was one of the most dramatic events ever covered on camera: naturally, it made an impression on us.

His daughter, Gina, was then 18: she has gone on to race and crash her own boats and set her own records. 'But I never thought I would follow him. I got married, and we were involved in horses, as a sport and as a business. I represented Britain in show jumping, and rode in point-to-points.

Divorce tends to make for violent changes in the way in which people approach life. Miss Campbell started power-boating after hers, and then, in October 1984, decided to have a crack at the women's world water-speed record. She talks about 'a genetic addiction to speed.' It killed her father and it came within an ace of killing her.

Speed has been the family business for three generations. Her grandfather, Sir Malcolm Campbell, set a world land-speed record in 1925 at 125 mph, and 10 years later he pushed the record back to 301 mph. Her father, Donald, took the world water-speed record to 276.33 mph, and he spent his life chasing more and faster records. It made a strange childhood for his daughter. Her parents were divorced when she was young and she stayed with her father.

'I lived with his plans, his successes and his failures. He thrived on success; failure sent us into doldrums of depression. I went round the world with him, and I learnt to love speed. I drove Formula Three cars when I was 15. When he died, I was working in a hotel in Switzerland. I was called to the telephone one morning, and before I answered it, I knew. I never thought water would kill him. And I never thought I would follow him.'

But this 'genetic addiction to speed' reclaimed her and led her to try for a new record in a new Bluebird. The Campbells call all their lethal speed-machines Bluebirds. This latest Bluebird was a Formula One powerboat, made for high performance and, as a result, highly unstable.

Miss Campbell spent a morning at Holme Pierrepont, Nottingham, learning the boat's eccentricities: 'At 75 mph it started porpoising, which frightened me. But it is just like a wheel-wobble on a car: you drive right through it. When you've done it once, you stop noticing it.' By the end of the morning, she was cruising at 100 mph. There is no speedometer in the boat, but the shore crew knew: greenfly do not stick to the visor of your helmet at lower speeds.

The time-keepers arrived in the afternoon, and Miss Campbell set about record-breaking. A record is set in two passes, one in each direction: because of the aerodynamic design, the boats go faster into the wind. Miss Campbell beat the record with triumphant ease: 122.85 mph. She did it so easily that the shore crew felt the boat had a bit more in her. So they removed the air-spoiler and Miss Campbell gave it another go.

'I did the 1,000 metres flat out, and then I just took off,' she said. Just as her father had done. 'It was a horrible feeling. Once you are out of the water, you have no control, there is absolutely nothing you can do. I was 40 feet up in the air, with the boat revolving around its centre of gravity, which is at the back, where the engines are. It twisted as it turned, and because of that, I was thrown out.

'It is only because I am so small that I came out so easily. I remember looking up at the sky as I came out of the boat, and thinking … "Shit!" Then I blacked out, and landed miles from the boat. The next thing I remember is the feeling of surfacing. I came up, and was able to swim towards my rescuers. Five minutes before, I had set a world record. Now I had written off the boat, and was lucky not to write off my body at the same time.'

But the Campbell way of dealing with such matters is to utter a light laugh and proceed to the next challenge. The family seems to like the idea of walking hand in hand with the great reaper and jumping skittishly clear as he swings his scythe. 'But I don't know if I would have the guts to try the water-speed record again. It would be different if someone were to take the record from me. I would like that, it would give me something to aim at. My father was a pure pusher-back of frontiers: I'm not. I like competition.

'I would like to go the same way as my father. Not a lingering death, not a "merciful release" death. I have a feeling that I will die a violent death. I don't want to get old ... but I don't want to die....' She gave a light laugh. 'There are so many nice clothes I want to wear before I go.'

DEFYING DEATH IS ALL IN THE DAY'S WORK
September 1986

Perhaps it is the jump jockeys who are the bravest people in sport. They do not, like some, face the real possibility of death[1] from their chosen game. That possibility is remote, indeed: the last National Hunt death was a decade ago when Doug Barrett was killed.

What they do face is the total certainty that they will get badly hurt. Last season the Professional Riders' Insurance Scheme received an average of 23 claims a week. Sooner or later, and again and again, absolutely no one escapes. They carry on in the face of these appalling risks simply by not thinking about them. But broken bones and concussion are part of the day's work and it happens to everyone. Absolutely everyone.

John Francome was luckier than most. Also, despite being champion and undisputed master of the sport, he gave up. Horses' names are always important, as everyone who has ever had a bet will reluctantly admit: Francome's last horse was called The Reject. 'It was one of only two occasions I had ever been terrified on a horse,' he said. The other was an insane bolter that carried him flat out over fences without any vestige of control.

But it was The Reject that ended Francome's career. In a bizarre and freakish accident his leg got entangled with the stirrup leather as he fell: the horse was set to continue his race with Francome pendant beneath. He wrote in his book *Born Lucky*: 'Geoff Capes wouldn't have been able to prise my fingers off the reins at that point. I knew that if the horse galloped off it would kill me.... The thought of what would have happened if he jumped a fence didn't bear thinking about.'

After an eternity or two people came to his aid and got him disentangled. 'I walked far enough away from The Reject so he wouldn't walk on me and fell to my knees on the grass. I didn't know whether to laugh or cry and settled for swearing out loud that I'd had enough of riding.' This was at the 1985 Cheltenham Festival. The next race was the Champion Hurdle; Francome surrendered his ride: the horse won by 10 lengths. 'I didn't feel the slightest pang of envy or jealousy. I was just thankful to be in one piece.'

He didn't give up then, not quite, but he did not forget it, and a short while later he had another fall: again on The Reject. This time he picked himself up and decided enough was enough. He has not ridden a race since, nor will he. Now, at 35, he is exploring other dangers instead, training Flat racehorses and jumpers from his newly established yard at Lambourn. 'I've never been superstitious but I felt then that it would be tempting fate to go on,' he said.

He went into racing in the beginning with the usual sportsman's blind faith that it would all be all right and had a winner with his first ride. With his second he broke his wrist. 'But it's a fact of life that you can't recall pain. At the time it's hurting you say you'll never ride again but as you heal you forget. You don't even think about it. Even when I gave up it wasn't that I'd lost my nerve. I couldn't have done it at all if I'd been frightened.

'But I know jockeys who are frightened. You see it every day. They've lost their nerve but they are still there because there's nothing else they can do. They don't give their horses a ride, they just go round. Win if they have to. Horses are funny things and they know. But it works the other way, too: when everything is in your favour and you are full of confidence it transfers to the horse. Always follow the jockey in form.'

Simply following Francome was always a good way of keeping ahead of the game. He collected a number of falls, broken bones and the rest, but somehow never received his fair share. A dislocated shoulder was the most painful. By the standards of jump jockeys this is nothing. He has been immensely lucky and knows it. A friend of his, Bob Woolley, is paralysed from the neck down after a racing fall.

'If you finish a race in one piece then the money is good,' Francome said. '£50 for a race, for four minutes' work, is good money: £50 for a broken leg is not. And the trouble is that there are too many jockeys, and many will go to a meeting for just one ride. They are taking all the risks but doing it for about £15 profit on the day. And they've got to do it, they've got to get their names up on the number-boards, accept rides on bad horses.

'I'd let a son of mine do it. Certainly. But not a daughter. I didn't let my wife, Miriam, ride in point-to-points. The reason is that for some reason women do not curl up in a ball and roll when they fall. So they get hurt.'

It is the Grand National that frightens outsiders the most with its monstrous fences and enormous fields. It is not quite as terrifying for the jockeys as spectators imagine. 'You get geed up for it but it's okay after the first half circuit, after everything has settled down. The start is suicide: some of them set off faster than they would in a two-mile chase. But when the blood is up you'll do anything, any stupid thing. Some owners are wonderful: as you go out, they say, "Good luck, look after yourself, look after the horse." A few, mostly enormous punters, are different.

'But, you see, jumping is a sport, unlike the Flat. The atmosphere is quite different at Newbury on Flat racing days. The parade ring is like a dentist's waiting room. On a jumping day everyone will be laughing and joking.'

Perhaps you can risk your own neck with a laugh and a

quip but when it comes to other people's money you must assume an edgy silence as a matter of respect. 'Race riding would be a perfect job if you never fell, but it is the risks that add to the excitement,' Francome says. 'And a jockey really does control his level of risk: watch Peter Scudamore. He is always in control. Other jockeys wrestle their horses to the ground, can't see a stride, can't anticipate the horse in front, can't find the room to see a fence … the lesser jockeys run the greater risks and that is compounded because they get given the worst horses.

'But risk is a part of the game you accept. You don't think about it. You might ride six races every day of a six-day week and you can't spend all the time thinking about the risks. But every time you leave the ground you're taking a risk. You know that but you don't think about it. You really don't.'

[1] I am sorry to have to write that two jump jockeys have been killed since I wrote this.

IN THE GRIP OF A TERRIFYING FORMULA
September 1986

Formula One racing is about power and money and death. Jonathan Palmer is a Formula One driver. He is also a Doctor of Medicine, though naturally he does not practise; he keeps a helicopter parked in front of his house, and naturally he flies it himself; and he is possessed by a demon. The demon's name is Ambition.

His ambition is more to him than any awareness of the dangers; his ambition pushes him out of reach of any doctor-like caution. 'It is ambition that brings you back to the grid each time. It is a kind of optimism; it is utter confidence in your ability; it is the belief that in the fullness of time you will be appreciated and rewarded. I am a great achiever. I set targets, and when I hit them, I move on. I drive myself hard; I am single-minded about achieving things; I take pleasure in doing things to the limit, in putting my ability to the test.'

Palmer drives for a new team called Zakspeed. His best this year has been eighth in Detroit and he was ninth at Brands Hatch. 'We started at the back of the grid and are now a third of the way towards the front. Soon we will be halfway: the team's progress curve has not slackened off.' Nor has his own. 'In this game, if you are not a star you have to be a rising talent. If you plateau off, your value falls, your shares slump, as it were, and you are out.'

Palmer came up through the formulae; he raced a frog-eyed Sprite as a medical student and during his 80-hours-a-week year as a houseman he raced every weekend. A not undetermined gentleman is Dr Palmer. On his way he has had four major smashes. The worst was when he crashed a Porsche head-on into the barrier at 130 mph, and broke his leg and his foot. 'I wasn't worried about losing my nerve. What worried me was that my foot might not work as fast after it had healed. But it was fine.'

The smash was caused by a sudden tyre-deflation. It is usually physical problems that cause the crashes. 'Formula One drivers are so good that there is scarcely an element of chance here. We control it. A driver setting a lap record is not constantly on the verge of crashing. But we drive at our absolute limits, so if something goes wrong with the car we are in trouble. Our safety depends on the strength of the cars.'

Colleagues have died; friends, too, have died on the track. It hasn't stopped him. 'It doesn't give me pause for thought, in that I might give up. It makes me angry. I feel sorry for the survivors, the family, but more than anything else, I feel angry at the unfairness of it all. Not angry at the car manufacturers, or the competition organisers ... angry at God, maybe. It is a pretty primitive reaction.'

The sport is hedged about with safety precautions, but people still die. Not often and not wantonly, but Formula One is still lethal: Elio de Angelis died after a crash while testing this year. 'It is safer than ever,' Palmer said. 'But it will always be dangerous. There will always be people who have limbs broken; there will always, occasionally, be people killed. We must strive to make the sport safer, while all the time striving to make it faster.'

The sport is dangerous because speed is dangerous, and because it is one of the most ferociously competitive sports ever seen. 'It is harsh, it is ruthless. There are 26 drivers on the grid at the start of a Grand Prix, and there's no room for any more to race. But there are another 30 drivers who believe that they should be out there. When someone is injured, even when someone is killed, these people rush for the phone.'

In Grand Prix racing, the dangers are surrounded, perhaps even enhanced, by enormous sums of money. The rewards for the men who make it to the grid are huge; the rewards for those at the front are unbelievable: Nelson Piquet is reputed to be receiving something in the order of £2 million this year.

'We all want all the money we can get – not just for its own sake, but because it is the measure of your success,' said Palmer. 'If one driver is getting £1.5 million a year, then it is everyone's ambition to be a £1.5 million driver. It shows what you are. But it is not money that brings you to the track. Money doesn't make you take impossible risks. But when people get killed, I feel we are worth the money.

'With 30 per cent of fatal accidents, I think, well, I would have been able to drive out of that one. But with the other 70 per cent, I know I would have had absolutely no chance. Every driver must admit that. And I think of the money, and say: well, I *deserve* this.'

No amount of money or glamour could disguise the bleakness of this world, in which ambition and danger are eternal bedfellows. 'I drive fabulous cars, which is very exhilarating, but I wouldn't call it fun. It is business. It is more about satisfaction than fun.'

Palmer is pursuing a vanishing dream at terrifying speeds, propelled by a 1,200 horsepower ambition. 'I have no idea what I will do when I finish racing. I enjoy life in the present. I don't plan ahead. I am striving; striving for perfection. The process of achieving results is not fun, and when you have achieved them, it is an anti-climax. The best part is the dream. In the reality, the pleasure subsides.'

But you can always find another dream.

ONE SINGLE FINGER FROM ETERNITY
September 1986

It is possible that Ron Fawcett is the sanest man I have ever met. On the other hand, it is equally possible that he is totally off his head. He is Britain's only professional rock climber, and he is only fully himself when 'I am holding on with one finger of one hand and two of the other and my feet are smearing on nothing.'

He is not one of your dogged ice and snow men. For such men, climbing is hard and bitter agony, and all that counts is getting there in the end. For Fawcett, climbing is a matter of extravagance and beauty, of brain and extraordinary physical skills pitted against the rock: a mixture of ballet, gymnastics, chess and sheer terror. He likes sun-baked rock, and more sun on his naked back; he likes climbs of the most fiendish difficulty and he likes to tackle them stripped to shorts and boots. He was one of the first people to train specifically for climbing ('before, if you didn't train on 10 pints and a packet of Woodbines, you were a nancy-boy'), and is so fit, in his specialised way, that he could do pull-ups with one finger if there was any point to it.

He certainly and regularly supports his entire weight on a single finger, 1,000 feet from the ground, from holds 'no wider than the edge of this pint glass': the very thought fills him with quiet delight. He has been well designed for climbing: tall and rangy, long-limbed and with hands like picks. He lives in the Peak District, naturally, and every day he is out there climbing. It is what he likes doing, it is what he is best at, and he doesn't ever want to do anything else.

He is a star among climbers, but that is not the point. He just climbs, and is filled with a sense of quiet delight. The best and the worst way to climb is by yourself; soloing. Just you and the rock; none of your ropes nonsense. 'There is no second chance. If you are off, you are at the bottom. Once when I was soloing in France, I got totally lost following a crack-line; up a 1,200-foot cliff with an overhang. Eventually, I got stuck. I was about 800 feet up. There was a bush, a tiny little thing, about 100 foot below me, and I was seriously considering letting go and trying to catch it. But I finally found a minute hold, and that gave me the inches to reach a bigger one. I was up to my neck, then.'

He retold all this in a calm voice in his local pub, as a mildly amusing yarn, rather as another man might talk of a nasty moment when he almost got out first ball. He is one of the easiest men you could meet, relaxed and gentle-mannered: 'I never liked team sports at school. A lot of climbers are the same. It is a very personal thing, climbing: you against the rock. With ropes, you fall, you get used to falling. But soloing, without ropes, is incredibly dangerous. You and your hands and your feet. You don't even fully control the risk: a hold could break, a bit of dirt on your boots could make you slip and you are gone ... but it is a charge, it really is. It is not something I do every day, but it is a charge. I used to think it was the best, but I've broken too many bones. And it is not fair on Gill.'

Gill is his wife, and a fine climber. Together they tackled a 2,700-foot climb in Yosemite National Park in California. It is meant to be a two- or even a three-day climb, but they went for broke and did it in six hours. 'You really have to go for it, and climb without any weight, any bags. If you are out there late, you're in trouble. But we did it.'

Climbing seems to groundlings to be the most terrifying sport of all: huge drops and hours on end to think about them, while muscles crack and nerves flicker and fray. Fawcett insists that he got frightened looking over the edge of the Eiffel Tower; Gill added that she wanted to throw herself off. Everybody does, but one would have thought climbers were immune.

Fawcett said: 'You climb so slowly, you get used to the exposures. And with climbing, it is not always the height that matters, it is the moving on the rock. Sometimes you can have a good achievement a foot from the ground. You can take hours to work out a route on a 10-foot boulder. Or a 70-foot climb might take you a week, working the moves out, piece by piece and finally putting them all together. That can be as satisfying as scaling a 1,000-foot cliff.'

What Fawcett loves is pushing back the frontiers, his own

102

and those of his sport. 'There are only personal rules in rock climbing, that is one of the attractive things about it. For example, you don't have to wear a helmet. I do when it seems sensible, but when you're climbing at your limits, a few ounces on your head interfere with your balance.

'Traditionally, British climbers believe that if it hurts, it must be good. They hate the way the French have fitted many of their faces with expansion bolts. These aren't to hold on to – I couldn't sleep at nights if I ever did that – but you can secure yourself to them and enjoy an extremely hard climb in relative safety. You can plot a route over days, and come off countless times, and in the end make a truly satisfying climb at the very limits of your ability.

'But you can never solo at the limits of your ability. With bolts you can do things like jump for a hold. If you come off, you can start again. The climbs are immensely testing and super-safe – and the French are harder climbers because of it. We are beginning to import the French ethic, and are collecting a lot of flak for it.'

Fawcett is a purist. His tastes for safe climbs and for ridiculously dangerous soloing are not contradictory. The pure dangers of solo climbing and the pure gymnastics of safe climbing are not exclusive: either way it is climber against rock; only the emphasis has changed.

'But risk does enhance it,' Fawcett said. 'There is the mental content: will you crack up on some massive rock with phenomenal exposure?' Gill said: 'We don't say, "Let's go out and dice with death this morning".' But they do it anyway. There is no hiding from the dangers.

The people who take part in these risk sports, these untrivial pursuits, are an impressive bunch: the parachutist, with his touch of mysticism; the Formula One driver with his vaulting ambition; Gina Campbell with her 'genetic addiction to speed'; John Francome with his honesty and his luck. But I think the only one I could actually envy would be Fawcett, who seems a man at peace with himself. All I spoke to were used to the proximity of danger and death, and are the richer for it. Only Fawcett had that enviable sense of quiet delight.

From the Diary

Serious measures to make pétanque, the game that smells of Gitanes and Pernod, a major sport throughout England are under way. A British firm has struck up a relationship with La Boule OBUT, France's leading manufacturer of pétanque boules. The new distributors maintain that they are not starting a new tradition for England, but reviving an old one. Francis Drake, they say, was not playing bowls at all on Plymouth Hoe. He was playing pétanque, or at least a game more like pétanque than bowls. For a start, they say, he was throwing a cannonball, and what is more, he could not have been playing bowls because the lawnmower was not invented at the time. The game of bowls as we know it simply would not work on a scythed lawn. Drake was playing on gravel: ergo he was playing a form of pétanque.

Here is my account of the best horserace I have ever seen or hope to see, and the best racehorse I have ever seen or hope to see. I was reasonably pleased with the piece, too, except that for some extraordinary reason *The Times* accompanied it with a photograph of the winning jockey, Pat Eddery, standing alongside JR from the television programme *Dallas*. One of the pleasures of compiling this book is knowing that JR will not be appearing in it.

ENGLISH ABSTINENCE FORGOTTEN IN ONE MOMENT OF SHEER DELIGHT
October 1986

Paris: The French would never have made a film called *Sunday Bloody Sunday* or even *Dimanche Bloody Dimanche*. When it comes to bloodiness, dimanches just aren't in the same class as Sundays. The Continental Sunday is traditionally a feast day. The English Sunday is a day of abstinence and gloom.

The English always feel a sense of liberation when they cross the Channel. This is not just because of traditional French seriousness about art, sex, drink and all the other things that Englishmen take with a sheepish grin; it is also because, in France, you have escaped the English bloody Sunday.

You could not have picked a better Parisian dimanche than the one just gone. It really was a feast day, a day of joy and celebration for all those who love the finest things in sport. It was the day on which a horserace was run: the Prix de l'Arc de Triomphe. And it was, without question, the finest day of sport I have seen this year, in reality or on television: it was better than the World Cup, better than the European athletics championships, better even than the day Tewin Irregulars beat BBC Children's Programmes. It was a Sunday quite shorn of bloodiness.

It was the horserace of a lifetime and, perhaps, the horse of the century. I shall not forget the way that wall of horses galloped into the final furlong, eight abreast, with eyes bulging, nostrils flaring, manes flowing and jockeys working like a set of berserk monkeys in their efforts to conjure something extra. The greatest sight in racing is that moment when, as all horses are going flat out, another cruises by as if the rest were standing still. Such magic is what racing is all about.

This is what happened. A horse went past that tidal wave of horses as if it were stationary. That was Bering, the top French horse, and what a fine horse, too; he found the extra gear, that almost mythical quality, the ability to quicken and then quicken again, which the men in the know call 'turn of foot'. It was a marvellous performance.

But even as he stormed past, there came yet another horse, a horse that possessed, unbelievably, impossibly, yet another gear. The ace of trumps was itself trumped by a power outside the rules; outside the rules, it seemed, of both physics and biology. A marvel was topped by a still greater marvel as Dancing Brave sped, like an arrow, to victory. It lifted the heart, it left you limp, it filled you with joy. And I didn't have a centime on the race, either.

Dancing Brave proved himself to be not just a champion, but, I think, a very great one. We will boast about having seen him. He has won the 2,000 Guineas, the Eclipse, the Diamond and now this. His failure in the Derby, in which he finished like a train in second place can, perhaps, be put down to the quirkiness of the Epsom track. I heard a theory, from one learned in horse lore, that Dancing Brave, unbalanced by the twists and turns at Epsom, changed his leading leg coming down the hill and, in that instant, lost the momentum he needed to catch Shahrastani before the finishing post intervened. Certainly, on sensible tracks, he has been unbeatable.

And on Sunday he ran a glorious race on a glorious day: a golden day of an Indian summer that was doing its best to make up for the proper summer that seemed to have been cancelled in early July. The Parisians were all gleaming in the sun, in beautiful condition as they strolled around the paddock, the women striving their utmost to outdo the horses; glossy, impeccably turned out, trained to a hair, glamorously connected and quite beautifully bred. The gentlemen, over-elegant to English eyes, wore chapeaux melon, dove-grey suits and looked like a bunch of understudies for Steed in *The Avengers*.

We are not allowed such treats in England, not on Sundays. On Sundays, the English must be bored, that is the law. The English Sunday is characterised not by the things you do, but by the things you don't do and are not allowed to do. People don't work, not because they have better things to do but because it is the Englishman's right and duty to be bored out of his mind all day on Sunday.

I am not speaking out in favour of the secularisation of Sunday. Far from it, and anyway, that has already been achieved. I am in favour of restoring Sunday as a feast day. Throughout the world, even in Lent, Sunday is a feast day. But in England, Sunday seems like a day of Lent in every season of the year. It has become a day of great poverty of the spirit. Because of this, I don't suppose there will ever be Sunday racing in England.

The English believe that racing is sinful, you see. Perhaps that is the secret of its appeal. I fail to see the sin, myself, in watching a marvellous horse performing deeds of wonder. People also believe that gambling is sinful. It is not even enjoyable. It is winning that is enjoyable. Mostly, gambling is an exciting way of making yourself depressed.

It was still an Englishman's dimanche last weekend. The race was invented in 1920 to celebrate the end of the war and 'to demonstrate the quality of French-bred horses vis-à-vis representatives of foreign breeding.' Mostly it has done just that. England had only won six before the weekend, Italy five, Ireland four and Germany one. The other 48 have all been picked up by the French.

Now, it is the custom among journalists to invent remarks 'overheard' in the crowd. I give my word that the following remarks from an unknown Frenchman are utterly genuine: 'Quel bel Arc!' he said. 'Quel jockey! Quel cheval! Phénomène!' It was a Sunday to treasure for ever.

The Hockey World Cup was one of the happier and jollier occasions of the sporting round. Of course, the game has advanced since then and has lost just a touch of its innocence in the process. There were a couple of rather unpleasant moments at the Seoul Olympics in 1988, though nothing that came from the players. But the game has been a discovery and a delight ever since Our Boys came out of nowhere in Los Angeles to pinch the bronze. They are nice people, and I wish them nothing but good.

ATHLETES FROM OUT OF THE UNKNOWN
October 1986

It is fitting that hockey's World Cup should be played at Willesden. It is one of those almost flamboyantly anonymous suburbs; a dull place on the way to somewhere else. On normal days, to arrive on the borders of Willesden is to have your spirits comprehensively lowered. But at the moment, Willesden is a golden country full of mythic dreams.

The English hockey team, ninth in the previous World Cup, have now won through to the semi-finals of the competition for the first time ever. The bunch of players that make up the England squad are having the time of their lives. There are even two people in the English team that your average sporting enthusiast could name instantly – Sean Kerly, the centre-forward, and Ian Taylor, the masked Michelin man in goal. These two are almost stars, and their team is almost taken seriously. For hockey, this is nothing short of a miracle. They are even appearing regularly on television; the stunningly gritty match against the Netherlands went out at 11.50 on Monday night, clashing with a Channel Four programme called *What Can I Do With A Male Nude?*

'This is one of England's greatest ever achievements,' said the coach, David Whittaker. 'This could be the take-off point for English hockey,' said the World Cup board chairman, Phil Appleyard. Perhaps so. In a way, though, one almost hopes not. The small-timeness of the game, the utter ordinariness even of its stars, is a cheering thing after the other World Cup held this year.[1] The great pleasures of Willesden make one cheer not just for hockey, but for the entire panoply of amateur sport.

One cheers for the unknown gym-teachers of the nation who work all day and then flog themselves into the ground every evening in pursuit of their dreams – the rowers and fencers and netball internationals, the canoeists and marksmen and weight-lifters. There are three teachers in the England hockey squad. 'The kids at school can't believe I'm an international sportsman,' Taylor said. 'They come up to me and say: "How can you teach and be an international sportsman?" There is only one answer, isn't there? With great difficulty.'

Taylor, undoubtedly a star in Donnington Road, Willesden, would be unrecognised if he moved as far away as, say, Uffington Road on the far side of the stadium. 'I've been the world number one goalkeeper in the assessment of the writers since 1978 and in Pakistan, I'm Ian Botham. Every time I walk out on the street, I'm surrounded. But if I go out to post a letter in East Grinstead, I'm no one,' he said.

Kerley is a transport manager. Imran Sherwani, the dashing winger who scored England's vital goal against the Netherlands, used to be a policeman, but he left the force to get more time for hockey. Now he is a newsagent. And a star, if his customers but knew it.

A star in a whizzing, hi-tech game. International hockey is played on plastic grass, and the ball runs away from you like a bar of soap in the shower. 'West Indian bowlers bowl at you from 22 yards at 90-odd mph,' Taylor said. 'In modern hockey the forwards hit the ball at you from 16 yards minimum, and at 160 mph. You don't get a lot of reaction time. And the ball is just as hard.'

The surface is hi-tech, and the goalkeeper's monstrous equipment must match it. This is a position only a lunatic would play in, but Taylor, comfortably domestic in East Grinstead, seems quite sane to the casual glance. He is just one of the legion of schoolteachers who, along with bank clerks, sports centre administrators, sports goods salesmen and many others, make up so much of the great ranks of British amateur sportspeople.

These are people with ordinary houses and ordinarily horrible mortgages. With pretty wives or handsome husbands, 2.4 children, and an 'A to B' motor car, one which is, in truth, slightly underpowered for all the travelling they must do to and from their training centres. They are quite ordinary, too, in that they have a dream that goes beyond their suburbs and their jobs. They get up at dawn to go and train, they drive for hours in the dark to reach distant places for team gatherings, they leave, normally with some reluctance, their loving families to spend weekends training and weeks touring. In the process, one or two get to the top, and suddenly and briefly, their sport catches the attention of the world outside. It gives all of us uncommitted millions a few moments of great excitement and pleasure.

The legion of unknown amateurs deserve our praise. If giving us pleasure is not their prime aim, it is certainly a by-product in which we all revel. The unknown men in the England hockey squad, Grimley, Clift, Shaw (teacher, bank clerk, sports goods sales manager) and the rest, along with all the unsung amateurs in every sport, deserve a song of their own. The song, incidentally, has already been written; Kipling is good at things like that:

'*Let us now praise famous men,*
Men of little showing,
For their work continueth,
And their work continueth,
Broad and deep continueth,
Great beyond their knowing.'

[1] The football World Cup in Mexico.

Here is more on flair and individuality v workmanlike professionalism – but this time, I have a scientific justification for it. I went to Lancashire to speak to the Great Britain Rugby League team, and read a book by John Syer, the sports psychologist (see page 55), on the train. With my head full of the book, I interviewed the team's individualists, and telephoned through the following piece.

ACES WILD FOR BAMFORD'S BRITAIN

October 1986

When Great Britain take on the awesome Australians tomorrow, they will be swept away if they show the slightest chink in their joint resolve. 'G'day, Maurice, how would you describe your team?' an Australian at the Press conference asked. 'Brilliant,' Maurice Bamford, the not un-bullish British coach, said.

They need to be. It is essential that Bamford has built that most elusive of things, a team in which the whole is mightier than the sum of its parts. Every coach tries; few succeed. And the memories of the last Australian team are still lucid in the minds of Rugby League men. They were reckoned to be the finest rugby team of either code to play in Britain. This new bunch want to be even better. Bamford has some task.

The boring way to accomplish it is to pack your team with the most solid of men, and to aim first at restricting the Australian score. You select the men who do what they are told and who never do much wrong. Or you can try and counter. You can add the flamboyant and the unconventional to the mix. This is the route Bamford has taken. Ellery Hanley is the spectacular runner, the man who can be a star and a disappointment on alternate days. Henderson Gill is the oddball: 'I don't play to a plan,' he said. 'I do what comes naturally.' This means ambling in and out of positions, turning up anywhere he fancies he might get a sniff of the ball. In short, a coaching nightmare. You just can't have an orderly and predictable game-plan if you pick a fellow like Gill. If you are particularly fond of game-plans, Gill is not the boy for you.

'I am so pleased the Great Britain coach has told me to play my natural game,' Gill said. 'I like to go hunting for the ball, you see. What I love is open space.' The season has been a treat for him so far: 'At the beginning, the Wigan coach told us all he didn't want robots, he didn't want to stifle flair. Well, my eyes lit up. And now I have my Great Britain shirt back as well. We'll be playing on a football pitch (Old Trafford), which is a bit wider than a normal rugby pitch. Give me a lot of ball on an open field and the opposition will be worried.

'The British coach has told me I can go wherever I like, so long as I am back on my wing when I have to make a tackle and, well, I agree with that really. But basically my philosophy is simple. I create havoc. I create havoc among the opposition, and I hope someone can capitalise.' To have such a person in your team is either a horror or a gift from the gods, depending on your own philosophy of havoc, or perhaps on whether Gill's instinctive wanderings have led him to a good day or a bad one.

Some coaches just can't bear the idea of nonconformism. But sports psychologists have pointed out that often the noncomformist is a vital part of the team. Not just in tactical terms, but also because the nonconformist helps create and maintain team spirit. Team members like an oddball, it helps with the jokes and it helps the team to define itself. It is an important role to play.

'Some research suggests that when a situation permits a person to be himself, to act freely and with integrity, his behaviour will be the most constructive and creative of which he is capable. It is when he is under pressure and goaded to be something other than what he is, to be alienated from himself that he is likely to become a problem personality.' This is quoted in a book on sports psychology, *Team Spirit: The Elusive Experience*, by John Syer, out next month. It makes one take a closer look at the way teams work.

Hanley is the most dashing of players, a flamboyant individualist, but he is also a team player through and through. 'I would not call myself unorthodox. What I have is match awareness. I use my instincts to set things up or to score. If you see a gap, you go for it.

'But the thing is that people always see the man who carries the ball. Me. People don't always understand that it is the forwards who win the match for you, and that I just finish it. They win the game, I get the glory. These grafters and workers and tacklers, they are jubilating with me when I score a try, but I am jubilating with them when they make a tackle.[1] I am saying, I wish I'd done that.'

These grafters, to quote Syer again, 'work hard in

training, do their best in matches, and yet in some way seem to drift along with events, without pushing their considerable ability to the limits. Not hungry enough to explore....

' "Many people dedicate their lives to actualising a concept of what they *should* be like, rather than actualising themselves," Perls said in *Gestalt Therapy Verbatim*. When they do this, they are more predictable and lack flair. Considered harshly, such conformity is a form of escapism, a settling for less than what one might otherwise achieve, when one is faced with a challenge of a hard struggle, of being different, or the risk of failure.'

True, it is likely to be as disastrous if you build teams entirely of wild individualists as it is if you build a team quite devoid of flair. It is the second error that coaches are more prone to, in just about every sport. Teams need a touch of wildness: 'Hanley is the most dangerous ball-carrier in the country,' Bamford said. 'He is a world-class player who has not yet gained the correct reputation outside Britain. He has been banished to the wing in internationals, things like that. God knows why. Now he is in the right place, and if he is on form, you Australians will draw your breath a bit. He has flair, he has an imaginative approach. He has just never been in the right shop window to impress you.'

Bamford sees the 1982 Australian tour as an equivalent to the traumatic visit by Hungary to English football in the 1950s. 'In the same way, it has forced us to take our heads out of the sand,' he said. The test for him, as for his team, comes tomorrow, when the world will see whether his classic blend of flair and solidity will do the business.[2]

Syer said: 'Some coaches don't want star players, believing that team spirit is based in equality. I think they are mistaken. The players may rightly be considered to be equal, but equal in diversity. To confuse equalness with sameness would be a mistake. You would lose team spirit by pursuing such a policy, in the act of trying to defend it.'

Modesty is considered becoming – how many football players interviewed after a match have said: 'It's really all due to the lads, Brian'? – yet some athletes have a natural positive arrogance which is far more exciting and presents a challenge

113

which can bring out the best in everyone.

[1] I love the word 'jubilating'. It is the perfect word for celebrating a score.
[2] Great Britain got stuffed out of sight when they played Australia.

This was a pleasant little piece to do. I include it for the sake of the pay-off line, which is one of the few jokes that made me laugh during the compilation of this book. Still, laughing at one's own jokes is not really a thing to be encouraged.

THE COLD DELIGHTS OF JUMP RACING
December 1986

Seeing that the last time I had been to the races was the Prix de l'Arc de Triomphe in Paris, it was time to go again. So on Saturday I went to Yorkshire and to weather-blown Wetherby to see the jump racing. It was different from Paris. For a start, I did not see a single man wearing the rosette of the Légion d'Honneur in his buttonhole.

The nearest you could get to such a statement of self-importance was to wear Hunter wellingtons and to eat your chips with your little finger extended. In Paris you could not walk past a single woman without being struck by the thought: how long did it take her to look like that? And how much did it cost? But Wetherby could have been filled with the most elegant ladies that Balmain ever dressed, and you would never know. It was too cold to look cool.

It goes a long way to explain why jumping will always be the poor relation of Flat racing; why the summer game has more status; and why all the really rich men love to plough their millions into the wired-up two-year-olds instead of the steady old fellas of the winter. In summer at the high and expensive meetings, for many the horses are no more than a mildly pleasant distraction from the serious business of gossiping and looking cool.

But there is absolutely no point at all in going to National Hunt racing unless you like actual National Hunt racing. It is simply too cold. You cannot look elegant when it is cold. You can look prosperous, true, but you have to dress to repel the cold, not to attract admiration. That wipes out most of the Royal Ascot crowd for a start. I didn't see them at Wetherby, anyway.

The horses are not the flickering chimeras[1] of the Flat racing season. Flat racing horses are babies, or perhaps to be more accurate, neurotic teenagers. Inciting them to go fast is like inciting a juvenile delinquent to break telephone boxes. They are seen for a season, perhaps two, and then never seen again. A thousand hopes and dreams vanish in a puff of smoke; several thousand more will appear next season.

But National Hunt horses go on forever. Surely that's not the horse I backed here five years ago? But it always is. Badsworth Boy, aged 11, was second in the big one (dammit). Well, you can't expect teenagers to have respect for traditional things like fences, can you? And fences can be vindictive if you do not treat them respectfully. Jumping horses go on forever – or at least, until disaster strikes.

The jockeys of winter are less flashy, less well paid and would all have problems getting a part in a pantomime,[2] being of a normal size. It costs no one much pain to make a weight of 12 stone. And they are probably the bravest sportsmen in the world.

A thumping, shuddering, crushing fall, the sort of fall a normal recreational horse-riding man would bore people about for eight months, and these men of steel get helped to their feet by the fence attendants, look about groggily, catch their breath, utter one heart-felt monosyllable and then hike back to change their shirt. There's another horse to fall off in half an hour.

Flat racing is glorious and mad. Jump racing has glory and madness of a totally different kind. Flat racing is slightly hysterical: jump racing is slightly dotty. There are those who see all racing as a sinful pursuit. If so, the sin of Flat racing

115

has the tang of satin sheets and silken clothes and exotic perfumes and curious cigarettes. The sin of jump racing is more like a tumble in the hay. And as with tumbling in the hay, it is always just that little bit too cold to be comfortable while doing it.

[1] This got into the paper as 'shimmerers'.
[2] Pantomimes were on my mind at the time – I had just seen my wife (an actress by profession) as Robinson Crusoe in the eponymous pantomime.

PART 5

THE TIMES 1987

Here is a piece on the art and sport divide. I had a few nice letters after this, including one that contained a reproduction of a Cubist scrum. It is nice to know that when you get a bit fancy, your readers are perfectly capable of keeping up. In fact, it's when you treat them like idiots that they lag behind.

TIME TO PUT SPORT IN THE PICTURE
January 1987

Tonight the Royal Society of the Arts is putting on a lecture called 'Offshore racing and the design of yachts.' Art and sport appear to have overlapped for the evening. It doesn't happen often. Perhaps that is a pity.

So far as painting is concerned, major artists have painted but two sports and ignored the rest. There are some marvellous pictures of horses and horseracing, starting with Stubbs and going on to Munnings, Degas and Dufy. Painters like Turner and van de Velde the younger have painted terrific pictures of yachts. But has any other sport been painted to any worthwhile degree?

When I talk about painting, I mean great painting. There are plenty of decent professional painters who paint things like cricket and golf, but they do not measure up to Stubbs any more than this column knocks *A la recherche du temps perdu* into a cocked hat. Yet there are plenty of things in sport I would like to see painted *brilliantly*.

One reason why they haven't done it is, of course, snobbery. Your average art critic considers that anyone interested in sport must be a mental gnome, a man who feasts on brown ale while he, the critic, drinks the champagne of the mind. Another reason is that sport has not always been available as a subject. A further reason is the modernist's fear of being intelligible. Sport is always obviously intelligible: you couldn't represent sport with a pile of bricks. Except perhaps Boycott's batting.

But real art can draw on anything, and anything includes even sport. And there are plenty of patterns and colours and, especially, movements that it would be wonderful to see captured by a Leonardo of cricket or a Michelangelo of track and field. Sport can possess ecstatic pictorial beauty as well as a grace of movement that begs for a master's eye. Damn it, the ancient Greeks sculpted sport, didn't they?

Ballooning is breathtakingly lovely to look at and fills the watcher with envy. *Ski Sunday* repeats identical shots for an hour and we watch it because it is so good to look at. A bowling green in summer has a delightfully peaceful and purposeful air. And snooker has become a number one television game because the pattern of the click-clacking colours are so pleasing to the eye.

I am not writing about horses and yachts here. They have had quite enough high art devoted to them already. And for a slightly different reason, I am not going to go on about the 'artistic' sports like skating. T and D were and are lovely, but they have always been consciously striving for loveliness. I am looking for moments when grace and beauty are by-products of some other sporting aim. Ed Moses is not striving to be beautiful; he just is.

Gymnastics and diving are on the borderline of 'artistic' and 'sport'. I am inclined to exclude them on the grounds that they are not really graceful at all. This is overstating the case rather: but high diving tends to be difficult rather than beautiful. A single clean lay-out somersault, slow and languorous – now that is beautiful. It is also, in sporting terms, easy. High divers do not hold pure lines, their concern is with eye-baffling turns and twists. They are not so much graceful as frightfully clever.

Gymnastics tends to go the same way, and anyway, I find the sport's obsession with little girls distressing, as I have said before. Lyudmila Turischeva, the last woman in gymnastics, she was graceful all right. And the gymnastics performed by men in their full strength are wonderful: the high bar exercises are a miracle of strength and grace. Michelangelo would have painted them rather well.

Athletics is a sport in which grace is often a by-product of achievement. I trust I am not being racist when I say that black athletes not only do most of it better, but they do it more gracefully than whites. True, there are few things more graceful than Cram high-stepping off a bend, but from Jesse Owen to Daley Thompson, it is the power and grace of black athletes that has given us the most perfect images of the sport.

The throwing events are more about power than grace, especially now the men throw a heavy, stubby javelin. But women still throw the spear that soars and defies gravity: Fatima Whitbread's victorious throws in Stuttgart last year were, from run-up to touch-down, stunningly graceful.

Horses and yachts have, as I say, been much painted. After all, people with yachts and horses can normally afford the odd painting as well: it makes better sense painting horses than whippets. But greyhounds are the most beautiful of creatures. Landseer painted Prince Albert's greyhound (who was called Eos, by the way) but sad to say, you don't get painters of similar stature at Hackney dogs. For dog racing can be a delight to look at. Ballyregan Bob, the new wonderdog, a tiger-striped brindle, is as paintable an animal as anyone could wish for, and the sight of six greyhounds racing in a line abreast will make anyone with eyes catch his breath.

Cricket is one of the prettiest games to look at and it has a grace all of its own. By rights I should be saying that Compton is the most graceful player I have ever seen. But as I was in a pushchair when I saw Compton in his pomp, my memory of his skills is a touch hazy. I wondered about Gower but it is not his grace that is pleasing. It is the fact that he does nothing at all – well, perhaps he moves his bat a few inches – and yet the ball goes scorching to the boundary. This is not grace but a conjuring trick. It pleases the mind, not the eye. No, the batsman whose sumptuous strokes have given me most aesthetic joy has been Botham. That straight drive of his, from its thundering start through to the wild exuberance of its follow-through, is a thing of beauty. It is not brute power: it is orthodoxy taken to an extreme with extreme results.

The bowlers' award for grace has a number of contenders. The snarling perfection of Lillee, the javelin-thrower's action of Thomson, the rampaging of Trueman in his prime: the finest fast bowlers are a gorgeous sight. But the most graceful cricketer that ever drew breath is Holding. Ah, that moment when he picked up his mark and reverted to his full run in the 1984 series and his soft, purring menace was unleashed. They called him 'Whispering Death' for two reasons: because the umpire could not hear the silent perfection of his run-up and because he was quite likely to kill you. I remember seeing a picture of Holding in one of his more regrettable moments kicking the stumps down: below the picture was printed the comment that no other cricketer could have committed so ugly an action with such grace.

Tennis is a game of dashing this way and that, chopping and changing and stabbing and slashing. The game is often delightful but it is seldom truly graceful. In fact, to be a graceful tennis player, you must be a person of quite extraordinary, if not unique, beauty of movement. Anyone who has not realised that I am talking about Evonne Cawley (née Goolagong) has missed a great joy over the years.

You might think that the more brutal the game, the less grace is involved. Of course, this is not the case. The contrast between the brutes trying to hammer someone, and the graceful genius who dodges them, has been a part of sport since Minoan times, and the sport of bull-leaping. The Romans placed gladiatorial combat on the same principle with *secutor versus retiarius*. American football works the same way. It is perhaps the most brutal sport of them all (I do not include boxing as a sport any more than I do cock-fighting) and yet it has moments of grace that few sports can match. Dan Marino, blitzed by a gang of brilliantly organised psychopaths, yet somehow unleashing one of those long, high passes into the end zone ... that is something.

Even ugly, muddy rugby has its moments when, despite all attempts by Chilcott and his like, a dashing, running poetry bursts into the game. I remember watching Fiji beat the All Blacks 28-0 in the final of the Hong Kong Sevens: men with the grace of panthers, the speed of stags, the strength of bulls, with arms like rocket launchers and hands like butterfly nets.

Even football has its moments of grace and beauty. No one could forget the sight of Best dancing through the clod-hoppers and turning his markers again and again. One of his bemused opponents was substituted 'suffering from twisted blood' as a colleague put it.

Indeed, sport – all sport – is full of beauty and delight. Those who have not noticed this, those who prefer a pile of bricks to a Stubbs, those who hold sport in intellectual and aesthetic contempt – well, let us note that they are missing a thousand treats, as anyone must if he walks around with his eyes closed, and let us leave it at that. Poor fellows: do they not see that every sport ever played has some kind of beauty and grace about it?

Except synchronised swimming, of course.

The Super Bowl is madder than you would believe possible. This is the final of the American football season, the greatest media bunfight in sport, the greatest hype, the greatest nonsense, and the most tremendous fun. This was the beginning for me of a great love affair with American sport. I cannot rationalise or justify this. I just like being lost in the middle of America with a ticket for the ball game in my pocket.

GIANTS RULE IN A WONDERFUL WORLD OF MAKE BELIEVE

January 1987

Pasadena: There were just over 4,000 media people accredited to the Super Bowl this year. Every year the media event gets a little bigger, every year it seems impossible that it should do so. The media headquarters for the event was the Anaheim Marriott, a hotel that is just a couple of blocks (if you will pardon this use of the vernacular) from Disneyland. I cannot believe that this is a mere coincidence.

The two weeks before the Super Bowl game is without doubt the craziest annual event in sport. And every year it gets crazier, just when you think it impossible it should do so. One thinks of the Super Bowl as a deeply entrenched part of American life, but the first Super Bowl was only in 1967. In that year, burglars broke into the headquarters of the Kansas City Chiefs and stole some money – but did not touch the 2,000 Super Bowl tickets. This year you could reportedly sell Super Bowl tickets for $1,500 (about £1,000) a go.

A memorable headline for the Super Bowl I read: 'Little Action Reported on Game in Las Vegas.' Very nice. This year, betting on the game was reckoned at $750 million legally and another $500 million illegally. My own gentlemanly and thoroughly romantic wager on the underdog Denver Broncos was an inevitable loser as the New York Giants ran out crushing 39-20 winners.

Back in 1967, the National Football League commissioner Pete Rozelle kept trying to tell the media not to call it the Super Bowl. Frightfully vulgar and populist, don't you know? The NFL had its *dignity* to consider. Now, of course, the Super Bowl has become the most gorgeously, sumptuously, ridiculously and splendidly vulgar over-the-top media event in the history of sport. That is obviously why they generally hold the event in Los Angeles. This year it was in Pasadena, which is not Los Angeles, nor yet is it out of it.

To arrive in Los Angeles is to lose your grip on reality, which obviously makes it a wholly appropriate place for the Super Bowl. There are 12 million people in Los Angeles, and

I don't think I have seen a single one of them walking. Nor do I have any idea where any of them live.

To travel around this place you get in a cab, and sit there for an hour, get driven along a 10-lane freeway packed with Californians in cars. Every yard you travel looks just like every other yard. You arrive eventually at a place which looks exactly like the place you've just left. The taxi driver will be awfully pleasant, ask you for 50 bucks, and then tell you (as if such a thing were still possible) to have a nice day. After spending $200 on wholly essential taxi rides in less than a day I felt my grip on reality slipping irrecoverably.[1]

On the whole, this was a help in covering the Super Bowl. But what got everything in perspective was visiting Disneyland. Without a shadow of exaggeration, Disneyland feels – is – more real than Los Angeles. It cannot help but feel more real than the Super Bowl.

The wonderful half-time entertainment at the match was produced by the Walt Disney Organization. It was called 'The World of Make Believe.' I tell you, Walt Disney is a master of understatement, an artist remarkable for his control and his earthy grip on reality, a positive virtuoso of austerity, when compared to the 4,000 people who bring the Super Bowl to the public.

Most of the questions at the amazing mass Press conferences are about the pressure that mass Press conferences bring to the players. Indeed, the remarkable thing is both the good humour and the articulateness of the players in the face of this tidal wave of silliness. The silliness itself is perfectly good-humoured. Everyone there understands how silly the whole thing is. This is not Disneyland, nor yet are we out of it. The whole occasion is terrifically cheerful, with a fizzing party atmosphere that reminded me, in a weird kind of way, of the Rugby League cup final.

For the supporters it was a pilgrimage and a jaunt and a great good time as well as a sporting event. The 4,000 media people themselves do not, for the most part, take it seriously. It is just the Super Bowl, an annual fortnight of craziness. There is no point in behaving like a British football reporter or television commentator, and pretend it is important for the future of the human race. To do so would be to spoil the party. It would pop the bubble as much as trying to be cynical would.

The ghastliest thing I have seen this week was a television programme that intercut scenes from American football with newsreel clips of American troops in Vietnam. The burden was of heroics and courage. Pass the sick bag. But a few minutes later I was hearing some American observer saying that American football is not like war at all. 'It's more like a cartoon,' he said. 'People get hit and smashed and chopped down – and then they get up and do it again.'

Practically all sport is a bit like that. It brings out great human qualities, but all the same it is a bit silly. The same man added that American football brought out the two greatest evils in American society – 'violence and committee meetings.' He enlarged: 'A load of guys jump on top of someone, and then they hold a meeting about doing it again.'

A third evil he might have mentioned is the media worship of sport. 'Blast the sports pages,' said Marshall McLuhan, 'purveyors of pickled gods and archetypes.' Indeed, when Mark Bavaro caught his touchdown pass in front of the posts and promptly genuflected and crossed himself as if he had caught a pass in front of the High Altar, it seemed that sport had finally promoted itself to man's prime method of coming to terms with the infinite.

The only surprising thing was that the game itself was, for the first half, a cracker. Two muffed field goal attempts by Rich Karlis saw Denver Broncos lose their will and let in New York Giants for their thumping win. Poor Karlis was in tears in the locker-room. This is a cruel game – like all games. And kickers in this game have a worse deal than most.

The golden boy, John Elway, quarter-back of the Broncos, sparkled and spluttered out in a welter of anxiety to overachieve, while a self-styled boring suburbanite, Phil Simms, quarter-back of the Giants, had a quietly emphatic and wholly decisive blinder. That he got the Most Valuable Player award was just and inevitable.

Once he and his boys got going in the second half, it became one-way traffic. The best team won – but at least they didn't do so too quickly. Also the media won decisively, as they do every year: The World of Make Believe, which is the heartland of sporting journalism, had yet another triumph. Disneyland is not just the heart of Los Angeles, it is also the global capital of sporting journalism.

And let me tell you, Disneyland is wonderful. As wonderful as the Super Bowl. There is no point in approaching either with a curled lip and a cynical gleam in your eye. You must simply revel in both, as glorious, delightful and uplifting nonsense. The Giants' coach Bill Parcells was asked to comment on a bout of sideline fisticuffs he once had with one of his players, and he put his finger on the pulse of the whole occasion. 'Listen,' he said, 'this is not a game for well-adjusted people.'

[1] Note this public justification of my expenses.

I have never really got the hang of the Cheltenham Festival. It is not a lucky meeting for many people, and never has been for me. I wrote this piece all about throwing money away on Budget Day. And because it was Budget Day and the system at the newspaper under some pressure, 300 words of this piece vanished, never to be seen again. But I still like what's left enough to include it, and besides, whingeing at technology is one of the modern journalist's professional pleasures.

PUTTING MONEY IN ITS PLACE – THE HANDS OF THE BOOKIES
March 1987

Budget Day is traditionally a day of ritualised and anguished avarice. It starts with the Chancellor's morning stroll, and then follows his procession with the great and sacred relic, the

Very Old Bag. Then comes the speech, and a nation that has been filling its tanks with petrol and buying Scotch by the crate now starts counting the pennies gained and the pennies lost. The day is a great celebration of all that is meanest in the human spirit.

But there was a small corner of England that had been insulated from all the gloomy pence-reckoning and petty gloating of Budget Day. A place where a nation's respect for almighty money was under the most severe threat: a place where avarice had been set in reverse. The place was Cheltenham, and at Cheltenham it was not Budget Day at all. It was St Patrick's Day and the first day of the Festival.

On Budget Day, the country traditionally demonstrates that it is totally in thrall to money. But as Humpty Dumpty said: 'The question is, which is to be master? That is all.' At Chelthenham, they know how to put money in its place. For the Festival is a great celebration of how the human spirit can conquer even cash. The people fling it away in buckets. The Irish save all year for these three days, and when they get here, they live like kings, drink like heroes, tip like gods and gamble like conquerors.

In the bus to Cheltenham, we had a chorus of *The Rose of Tralee* before the wheels started turning, and the pubs were not even open. Indeed, the singers, with great bushes of St Patrick's Day shamrock dripping from hats and lapels, were not even drunk. They were simply happy: sober and happy. I hoped that only one of these conditions would be altered by the day's event. Galmoy won the fourth for Ireland, so life cannot seem all that bad this morning.

But, I hear you say, racing is all about money. True. Surely, then, racing is in fact a vast outbreak of mass avariciousness, an unsightly rush to get something for nothing? But this is wrong. Betting is mostly about losing. Indeed, I am sure that if you were to walk through Tattersall's today carrying a large green bin and a notice that read: 'Please do not put money in this bin,' you'd be a millionaire before the fifth race.

Betting at Cheltenham is a mass celebration of anti-avarice, and an expression of total contempt for the Protestant ethic of careful husbandry. People shove, push and fight like fury in their efforts to get rid of the stuff, to force their tenners into the ever-willing palms of the bookies, while above their heads the tictac men perform their Balinese finger-ballet as they direct the never-ending flood of money from shamrock-wearing punters to Honest Solly and Co in the ring.[1]

[1] I repent of this. Many bookmakers are, indeed, Jewish, but the line is gratuitous.

One of the pleasures of pontificating about sport is the freedom to go on the occasional rant. I have completely failed to understand the point of the America's Cup. I find it as loathsome as it is tedious. And so when I was sent to cover a Peter de Savary Press conference, I went there with a nasty look in my eye, and ended up with the following few words of mild and restrained criticism.

HOW TO MIX A COCKTAIL OF HYPE
April 1987

Just when you thought it was safe to get back into the water, the America's Cup business has started all over again. A British challenge for the next competition was announced yesterday by Peter de Savary, who is, of course, Britain's yachting superstar. Not that he is actually a yachtsman, of course. He is a businessman, and a particularly shrewd example of the breed. But the stars for the America's Cup are always the businessmen, and not the sailors. This makes excellent sense, given the nature of the event.

So there was de Savary, with his bottle of Bollinger and a cigar the length of a stick of Brighton rock (it probably said 'I am rich' all the way through) at yesterday's Press conference. He is vice-chairman and chief executive of the Blue Arrow

Challenge: the chairman is Tony Berry, who is also chairman of the sponsoring company, Blue Arrow. Even non-City people have now heard of Blue Arrow, because of their telly ads.

The most important sporting fact we learned yesterday was that the challenge will cost £10 million. Berry went on to tell us what excited him about 12-metre yacht racing and the America's Cup. 'At first I didn't think it was right for us ... then I saw the amount of media publicity the event received.'

So *vive le sport*. They plan to spend £4 million on research and development, and will build four, or maybe five, boats in their efforts to make a good 'un. They also told us, in their sporty way, the number of important yachting people they had 'got' for the syndicate. 'We were looking for a vehicle to promote our name,' Berry said, and unveiled a picture of a vehicle. The picture shows a yacht, and it was apparently painted by Grandma Moses, but it says BLUE ARROW on the sail very large indeed: I don't know much about art, but I know what I like.

As Blue Arrow dream on about a fibreglass-hulled billboard, it cannot be denied that the America's Cup is a fascinating phenomenon. But it is not the sport that makes it fascinating. It is the money. The power, not the glory. It is a battle between rich men who are hurling 100 dollar bills at each other. De Savary has said that his 1983 campaign cost £3.5 million, but that he made three times that in deals he was able to set up because of the stardom − perhaps he would prefer the word 'profile' − given him in America by the America's Cup.

'The America's Cup is the third largest event, after the Olympic Games and the football World Cup,' Berry said. 'With sponsorship and profile it could become *the* largest.' Well, here is a quiz on how large the event is in the public mind: only non-yachting people may enter. *Question*: How many America's Cup skippers can you name? *Answer*: Dennis Conner, and well, that New Zealand chap, and ... er ... No, I suppose Alan Bond is something else, isn't he?

But we all know that the America's Cup must really be a great and fantastic spectacle, because we have been told it is.

Again and again. So many millions have been spent by sponsors and various bits of the media that these people are now convinced that none of us can resist the lure of 12-metre yachting. They daren't believe anything else.

But the truth of the matter is, as we all know, that 12-metre yachting is not interesting at all. As a matter of fact, it is extremely boring. The blood of the uncommitted will never be stirred by tackling duels. Darts makes much better television. The truth is that the public has become the victim of a huge confidence trick. The enthusiasm of the media for its latest creation, the America's Cup as mega-event, has created a massive illusion of public interest.

Such public interest as there is, is wholly superficial, probably temporary and is no more than a media-created phenomenon. The America's Cup is surfing on a totally bogus wave of global interest. Only the money is genuine. Meanwhile, we keep being told that the America's Cup is the new king, the new emperor of sport. True, this emperor is rich and powerful beyond all imagining. But tell me: why isn't he wearing any clothes?

From the Diary

Alan Knott, the Kent and one-time England wicket-keeper, makes it quite clear in his autobiography, *It's Knott Cricket*, that he is a stand-up-and-be-counted Christian. He goes on to say: 'An example of the Lord's guidance came for me with my decision to join Packer's World Series Cricket.' It had not before occurred to me that the ways of the Lord were quite that mysterious. I am proud to report, however, that last Sunday the rector of St John the Baptist, Chipping Barnet, led a Congregation XI to victory over a Choir XI between lunch and evensong, thanks to his devilishly cunning captaincy.

A further example of the advantages of being a columnist: I went to cover an ice hockey match, and went spiralling off into a moral debate. My colleague, Norman de Mesquita, wrote about the hockey: me, I had another stab at writing about the meaning of life. As an old friend of mine is wont to say, *chacun à son guru*.

UNWRITTEN CONVENTIONS BEAR THE WEIGHT OF OUR FOIBLES
April 1987

When you watch an unfamiliar game, it is important to get the hang of the rules. I went to the ice hockey final this weekend; I found it a grand, raucous occasion, but the rules were a mite elusive. This is a game of exuberant physical contact, I know, but is the elbow in the throat a legal tactic? Is the stick-end in the ribs permitted in the rules? And when half a dozen chaps pile into each other with fists flashing, and all end up in a dirty scrum in the middle of the ice – is this part of the game's permitted cut and thrust? For certainly all these things went by without incurring punishment.

The point is that the rule book is not much help in learning what is and what is not permitted; there is scarcely a game played in which the rules are kept. Games are governed not by their rules, but by conventions of what is acceptable. Referees and players all adhere to this unwritten code, and not to the book of rules.

'The art of refereeing, as I learnt very quickly in my career, is knowing what not to call,' my colleague, Norman de Mesquita, a former ice hockey referee, wrote in the programme to the final. 'Just imagine what sort of game you would get if the referee called every single infraction without any discretion whatsoever.' In other words, it is the conventions, not the rules, that count. In rugby, it is accepted that a reasonable amount of aggressive cheating in the lineout (normally referred to as 'argy-bargy') is inevitable: part of the game. If the referee applied the rules as written, he would blow his whistle every time the forwards contested any ball on the field. The result of this is that the first 10 minutes of every rugby match are spent sizing up both your opponents and the referee, to define the exact scope of the conventions you are playing under.

There is something of the same thing in football. Just about every action picture with two players in it shows some kind of sub-legal grappling and fending-off. It is a convention that defenders are allowed to foul *just a little bit* in the penalty box, presumably because to penalise them with a virtually certain goal would seem a bit rotten.

In cricket, the conventions have got ravingly out of hand. The Laws state that: 'The bowling of fast, short, pitched balls is unfair if, in the opinion of the umpire at the bowler's end, it constitutes an attempt to intimidate the striker.' Well, all serious bouncers are intended to intimidate, and when some non-batter is involved, as in Malcolm Marshall's famous spell at Pat Pocock, the contravention of the Laws is absurdly obvious. But by current convention, it is cricket.

It is not just the games of physical conflict that operate in this way. In tennis, it is a rule that a player must serve within 30 seconds of a point being scored. So take a stop-watch to one of the leading tennis players when he has dropped a point on his service. There always seem to be just a few extra seconds to regroup himself and to disrupt his opponent's rhythm: but nothing too defiant. So it is reckoned to be okay.

The elasticity of the convention is often directly related to the player involved. Kenny Dalglish is permitted a certain amount of obstruction as his due when he is 'shielding' the ball; fouling George Best was always a less heinous offence than fouling Bobby Charlton: 'The other players daren't kick him, because he was like a bloody national institution,' Best said. Indeed, a top referee once referred to Norman Hunter as 'an honest clogger'; which is rather like describing a Mafia hitman as 'an honest murderer.'

Sport is, some people like to think, something that teaches moral standards. Of course, it does no such thing; it reflects the doubtful morals and approaches of the society it is played in. In real life, in conventional circles, it is wrong to punch people in the face at a cocktail party, but perfectly okay to drive home drunk and risk killing someone. The lesson sport teaches is that there are certain things you cannot get away with, and that there are other things, no less pernicious and no more legal, that are perfectly acceptable. For there is nothing in the world quite so unsporting as sport, unless it is real life.

From the Diary

Sport is the ultimate trivial pursuit, but is Trivial Pursuit the ultimate sport? Could there be a more trivial pursuit than Trivial Pursuit? Willow Enterprises have made a valiant bid to create one with Cricketrivia, a board game built on the as-yet-undimmed craze. It includes 4,000 questions on matters of vast importance related to the game of cricket. Here are four.
1 Where is Corporation Stadium?
2 How many Test wickets did Keith Fletcher take?
3 Who was F. S. Jackson's fag at Harrow?
4 Who said: 'Cricket? It civilises people and creates gentlemen. I want everyone to play cricket.'
  Answers: 1 Madras. 2 One. 3 Winston Churchill. 4 Robert Mugabe.

This is evidence of my growing warmth towards Steve Davis. I wrote about how emotional he is: on a recent television programme he was caught blubbing at Tessa Sanderson's emotional reaction to her gold medal ceremony in LA. 'It always sets me off,' he said, wiping his eyes and laughing. 'I always cry at *Lassie* an' all.'

132

DAVIS LETS THE MASK SLIP

May 1987

Steve Davis is not the sort of chap you associate with emotional excesses. But on Monday night, after winning the world snooker championships, he was in absolute floods. He came to the compulsory Press conference afterwards with his eyes more red than his hair. 'Yes, it's a very emotional occasion,' he said, and the word 'emotional' almost set him off again. It took a quite heroic effort to will the tears back into their ducts again.

And he went on to speak about the emotional stresses of snooker. Can this be the man who sets his mouth into the shape of a circumflex and the rest of his face into a death mask, and who marches about the table with such rigid, controlled and easily-parodied movements? Well, yes it is, actually: only an emotional man would require so elaborate a defence against emotion.

This is a game that lays the emotions bare for an audience of millions: we get every twitch in close-up. He who twitches least wins most: Davis has schooled himself not to twitch, has invented this man-in-the iron-mask defensive technique. And it has taken him through to the recovery of his world title after two traumatic finals: Dennis Taylor beat him on the last black, and then Johnson demolished him last year.

'This tournament is so difficult to win,' Davis said. 'You never know what will happen, and you never know when you will fall apart on the table. And you do fall apart – I know. I fell apart twice during the final. Two times, the world caved in on me. And you've got to come back from it. Don't lose your mind: you've got to try and get it back together again on the table. I managed to do that both times. I'm very proud of that.

'People might think that it is easier to win the world championship if you've won it before, if you've been in the final the year before. But it's not. It's easier to panic. Having been beaten the last two times – oh, it's horrible, getting beaten in the final. You go blind, it all comes at you, you say: "Oh no! Please don't let it happen!" I am very proud to have

133

played so well with that over me. I did play really well. I played fantastic.'

Well, he did play rather fantastic. Last year, as Johnson played inspired snooker, Davis retreated fearfully until he was playing an absurd caricature of his own game. He played the safety option time and again, with possible pots open to him. He turned his own desire for victory into a potent weapon against himself. He would eye a long pot, think 'What if I missed?' and lay up as safe as he could. And Johnson would thunder in a length-of-the-table pot and start break-building again.

But this time, Davis was attacking the long pots, the long pots that let a player in amongst the balls, and he was smacking them down with gusto: 'I knew I was going to get those long ones,' he said afterwards. 'Even before I got down over the shot, I knew the pots were going to go in. It's nice to have that feeling, the long potting was the key to the game – in fact, the worst aspect of my game this time was the safety.'

This was Davis unchained: his play was certain, decisive, and, in the end, there was no answer to it. Johnson played some magnificent stuff, fighting back with four successive frames to crowd Davis and let anxiety do its evil work. But it didn't quite work. 'You've got to be prepared for this tournament, prepared for anything,' Davis said. 'You know – like the boy scouts.'

People like to believe that Davis is 'boring', but actually they are wrong. Davis is fascinating. He has something in common with Bjorn Borg: both are legends of remorselessness. But Davis has been cracked and broken twice in the tournament that matters, and this time he has come back to win it, and win it with an air of inevitability. This is not boring: this is remarkable.

When Davis has taken off his match-day iron mask, he is a jolly, affable, pleasant chap, the sort who likes to make little jokes, like the one about the boy scouts. He is also, unlike many professional sportsmen, in love with and absolutely fascinated by his own sport: both the technicalities and the emotional demands of the game enthrall him. He brings the power of a very sharp, perceptive and honest mind to mastering both aspects of a game that requires such immense emotional and technical resources.

The popular view of Davis is of a man with a vital piece missing: that he is only half a human being. And people like to compare this with what they see as the emotional richness of a man like Alex Higgins. But what is striking about the Higgins saga is its desperate emotional poverty. His snooker is vivid and beautiful: his life is not colourful at all. It is drab and depressing beyond belief.

Davis is, in fact, a much more unusual man, a much more, dare I say it, *interesting* person. It is the strength of his will that is so intriguing: the way he has done his best to turn himself into a machine that makes victories. And on Monday night the machine wept.

Another torrent of praise for Glenn Hoddle. I did write that he always lets you down when you least want him to. This was written as a preview to the Cup final. Coventry City won, and Hoddle did his classic disappearing act.

STANDING IN THE FIRING LINE IN DEFENCE OF HODDLE'S SKILLS
May 1987

I sometimes have moments of terrible vertigo in the Press boxes of football grounds. At the end of the game, I will hear two wise football journalists in conversation: 'For me, Bumstead was man of the match.' 'Didn't put a foot wrong, did he?' And I feel a dizzying rush of confusion overwhelm me: Who the hell is Bumstead? Which side was he on? What did he do in the game?

There is a place in life for solid, steady, professional virtues. When you are at work, for example. But when I go to a football match, I want something else. Genius, glory, inspiration, beauty, joy. All that sort of stuff. When you *play* football, you are happy to mark tight, play 10 at the back, and win by a single fluked goal. But when you watch: well, you want something more. At least I do.

And so for years I have carried the burden of being the most devoted admirer of Glenn Hoddle. To confess such an affliction in a serious footballing conversation would always bring a great chorus of pshaws and bahs, and will also bring you hours of vilification. 'Hoddle doesn't tackle, Hoddle doesn't get stuck in, Hoddle doesn't chase and harry, Hoddle doesn't defend well, Hoddle is inconsistent.' To all this, I say 'Fiddledeedee!'

Brian Clough is the man to have beside you in an argument about football. 'You don't have to bare your false teeth to show you are a real he-man in football,' he said. 'Some people are morally brave, and Hoddle is one of them. I've heard him criticised for non-involvement, but I'm not sure what that means. If you can compensate with more skills in one foot than most players have in their whole body, then that is compensation enough.'

Hoddle himself says: 'Unlike the Brazilians, we start looking for faults as soon as we recognise a player's skill. I've had it pushed down my throat ever since I was a kid. Of course, the runners and tacklers are part of the game, but people don't have a go at them if they can't play 40-yard balls or go past three men at a time. They don't expect them to do the things skilful players are good at ... that is the way we are in England.'

There is a great mistrust of the exceptional in British football, or maybe I mean in Britain. There is a great worship of mediocrity: the most loved heroes are the ordinary blokes who make good by playing within their limitations. I think the ultimate British sporting hero was David Steele, the mild, bespectacled batsman who looked like a grocer, and who was drafted in from nowhere to defy Lillee and Thomson. His wonderful heroic competence delighted us.

But an athlete of outrageous talent is, in Britain, someone waiting for his come-uppance. Someone who is so sharp he will cut himself. In the morality tale of George Best's Progress, it slowly became clear that Best was not villain but victim, that the public were not his audience, but his enemies. He was skilful and wondrously gifted, and the world willed him to fall.

Go to a football ground and hear the great crows of pleasure when Hoddle, or Nevin, or Barnes, tries to go past a man and blows it. A great bay of delight echoes round the ground. That'll teach him to be clever. As Duncan Mackenzie, another man gifted with almost voluptuous ball skills, once said: 'The attitude in England is the tricks are okay if they work. If they don't, you're an idiot. It doesn't seem to have sunk in that if you never try, you'll never succeed.' I don't think Mackenzie goes far enough. If you try tricks at all, even if they come off, you're an idiot, and you deserve what comes to you. You deserve it when some manly chap comes chopping you down from behind. That's *real* football for you.

One imagines that if Hoddle had been anything in the world except British, he would have been cherished and made much of in everything he did. On the field he would have been protected like a quarter-back. Club and international teams would have been built round him from the start. Instead, his England career has been, until recently, an in-out thing. He was played often tentatively and in incongruous positions: people said afterwards: 'See! I told you he wasn't an international!'

Of course, Hoddle doesn't help his admirers all the time. His temperament is, for all his arrogant moments, rather diffident. He likes to hang around outside the penalty area when the ball is pinballing around inside, waiting for a chip shot. He is not an up-and-at 'em sort of chap and games seem sometimes to overwhelm him.

But Hoddle will always make it up to you. It is remarkable that England have such a fine player: the whole tendency of the British game is to shut up such players before they get started. Hoddle is not like an English player at all: but for all that, he is a very English sort of chap. Diffident, as I have said, not pushy. He has talked about playing 'in Europe' for ages; indeed, he has played his last game for Tottenham on several occasions. But he has never quite gone.

On Saturday, he could be playing another last game for them. He has had a new burst of enthusiasm for the notion. He senses that this is his last chance for such delights: perhaps even now he has left it too late. He is 29, and not, perhaps, the most obvious investment for a major club. Paris Saint-Germain are the latest club to have a think about him: we shall see. No one will be 100 per cent surprised if he is playing another last game for Tottenham next May.[1]

I rather hope that this is the case, because I love watching him play. I love the way that those who worship mediocrity can be made to shut up by a single open-sesame path. There is a football team that lives quite close to Tottenham whose supporters seem rather obsessed with efficiency: with organised mediocrity.

Danny Blanchflower once said: 'The great fallacy is that the game is first and last about winning. It's nothing of the kind. The game is about glory. It's about doing things in style, with a flourish, about going out and beating the other lot, not waiting for them to die of boredom.' Amen to that. And no danger of it happening when Glenn Hoddle is out there and when he is playing like Glenn Hoddle.

---

[1] It was his last game for Tottenham. He moved to Monaco, and has done well there. In 1988, he won the French Best Foreign Player award, the first time an Englishman has done so.

This is a piece for the same Cup final (see page 135). It is about Cyrille Regis, who somehow never quite got to be a *great* player. In fact, it is mostly about the emergence of the black footballer. Regis has remained perpetually promising, perpetually on the threshold of great things – but in the Cup final he played a blinder, and was for most people, myself included, man of the match.

REGIS: AN ENIGMA WITH VARIATIONS
May 1987

Does this take you back? 'I don't care if he's black, white or yellow with purple spots. If he can do a job for me, Brian, then he's in the team.' It is what football managers who selected black players used to say on television in the 1970s. At the same time, the managers who did not choose black players said, though not on television: 'The trouble with black players is that they've got no bottle, no heart. Right?'

Now, of course, it is impossible to imagine football without black players. Big bruising centre-forwards, flying wingers and also, to confound the expectations of the ignorant, calm, solid defenders and even a goalkeeper. Viv Anderson is England's regular right-back and John Barnes almost saw off Argentina when he came on in the 'Hand-of-God' match last summer.

The tide turned for black players when Ron Atkinson selected three of them for his dashing West Bromwich Albion side. Naturally, they were called the Three Degrees – Brendon Batson, Laurie Cunningham and Cyrille Regis. Regis came from non-League football and, in his first First Division match, he scored with a run from the half-way line. Surely, we all thought, this would be the first black player to play for England; surely, he could be England's centre-forward for years; such skill, such speed, such power, such confidence. Yet he has played for England just four times.

Anderson was the first black England player. Regis went from West Bromwich to Coventry City. Coventry! On Saturday, he plays against Tottenham Hotspur in the FA Cup final. Ludicrously, this will be the biggest match of his life. Yet he could have done so much more.

His appearance has always been against him. He is beautifully put together, packed with bouncy muscle, and he looks like a boxer right down to the scar tissue around his eyes. He looks mean and pugnacious – a black battering ram of a player who runs straight through people. But he doesn't play like that at all, which throws people – especially those disconcerted people who, right from the beginning, found the idea of black people playing football difficult to accept. Regis did not live up to their clichés.

'People say I'm not aggressive enough,' Regis says. 'Well, there are two ways of expressing aggression. One is to go physically straight at your opponent and the other is to beat him with the ball. I'm the second type. But, because I look tough, people expect me to play like an Andy Gray or John Fashanu.' The scar tissue comes from accidental clashes of heads, not fisticuffs.

Regis is an enigma, in so far as he does not look like the player he really is – neat, swift, explosive and intelligent. Years ago, C. L. R. James scoffed at 'the persistent illusion of West Indian spontaneity' as if thought, intelligence and planning could not possibly be the explanation for West Indian excellence. Nobody doubts that this is the case now. And, in football, the growing numbers of black players have begun to destroy the notion that they are either bruisers or flash-boy runners – all muscle and no brain or all speed and no brain. The calmness and good sense of Anderson's style has done a lot to lay those myths.

But, somehow, it has never worked out for Regis. 'I think I have always been a yes-but player in people's minds,' he says. 'They always look for negative things in me. They don't look at my strength – only at my weaknesses, to what they see as my lack of aggression. What I have that is extra is that I can give people that run of excitement. I'm like Hoddle or Barnes. Something always *might* happen when I'm on the ball.'

Like many a rising player, Regis was injured at the wrong time and has since always been seen as yesterday's player: people in football can be as fickle as newspapers. He had two years with about 30 games and 'a succession of niggles' and, after that, the then manager of West Bromwich, Johnny Giles, decided to cash in while the going was good. They sold him to Coventry for £250,000.

'I was sure the big clubs would come in, but they didn't,' Regis says. 'I thought: "God am I worse than I thought?" And then, in the end, I said: "Right, then, all right. I'll *go* to a little club. I'll go to a little club and build it up. I'll show them who's missed out." ' If you can call performing miracles to keep Coventry in the First Division 'showing them', he has done that all right. And, this season, Coventry have started to look like a football team.[1]

For once, Coventry haven't got to worry about relegation. 'And I'll tell you something else,' he continues. 'We haven't lost the last game of the season for three years. Pressure? When we had to beat Stoke City, Luton Town and Everton to stay up, that was pressure. Last year, we beat Queen's Park Rangers to stay up. Three years ago, it was Norwich City.' This time, it is Tottenham – and not for survival. This time, it is for glory.

All black players – and, indeed, everyone who enjoys football – owes a debt of gratitude to the barrier-breakers. To Regis and Anderson and Atkinson and the Three Degrees. In my optimistic moments, I think the emergence of black footballers has been a good thing for the nation. But Regis has not gained all that he might have from the deal.

He has dual nationality, having been born in French Guyana, and had an offer from St Etienne. Perhaps he could have been France's centre-forward for a decade. Certainly, he is more their sort of player than ours – skilful, I mean. Regis has given pleasure out of all proportion to his rewards. Perhaps the fates owe him a day of glory.[2]

---

[1] Regis said he couldn't bear the thought of life without the joys of team spirit, the pleasures of team games. 'I suppose I'll end up a fanatic member of a bowls team or something,' he said.
[2] Well, he got it.

Here is another story which must remain dateless. I can't even remember the year, but it was written in response to various pieces on the decline of school sports, and all that 'something must be done to safeguard the international superstars of the future' argument.

SKIVING OFF WITH *FINNEGANS WAKE*

The more I read about the decline of sports in schools, the more I remember the Wednesday afternoons of my own youth. I used to love games afternoons more than anything. Ralph and I used to go to the pub, and drink halves of Watney's Starlight and discuss world revolution and whether *Finnegans Wake* was better than *The Rainbow*.

The people who played games were miles beneath our mountainous contempt. We called them 'the bruisers', made self-regarding 'intellectual' jokes about them and changed the subject to *Les Evénements* in Paris. That, along with girls and looking cool, was a subject more worthy of discussion.

This was because, before the discovery of Starlight bitter, games afternoon had been an unmitigated horror for five years. Schools rugby seems to be a sport designed to give a supernatural advantage to those who reach puberty spectacularly early. For just about everybody outside the year's top XV, rugby was a muddy, freezing nightmare of aimless uncoached running about followed by intricate tactical manoeuvring whose purpose was to avoid having a shower.

Though my school was pretty keen on cricket, I never got to play at all. I suspect this was because I was bad at rugby. I was okay at cross-country running, but I gave this up after I had, for some freakish reason, run so well I beat the field home by more than a minute. The teacher then refused to tell me my time because it was so fast 'it was obvious I had taken a short cut.' School is supposed to teach you that life is unfair, but that was the end of cross-country running for me, and that was also how the nation lost a great athletic star.

I coxed eights briefly, but with fairly disastrous results. I had the great pleasure of re-meeting my old coach recently, and reintroduced myself as 'the worst cox ever seen on the Tideway.' 'I have known worse than you, as a matter of fact,' he said, 'though the competition for that honour is pretty intense.'

The school tradition of games gave me an awful time, in short. I hated games. So did practically everybody. The

142

fatties, the skinnies, the shorties, the uncoordinated, the myopic, the uncompetitive. The only competition was about who could get an aegrotat for some trifling ailment and thus spend the afternoon mucking about.

However, far more important than its belief in games, the school had a noble tradition of tolerance. Ralph and I, Wednesday afternoon 'intellectual' skivers, were accepted as part of the school's and life's rich pattern. An official blind eye, I suspect, was turned to any suspicion that skiving involved the sins of Starlight bitter.

Sport was something I despised. Since then, sport has become one of the great pleasures in my life. I play cricket throughout the summer with huge enjoyment, even if the lack of early coaching is apparent in every movement. I ride by horse as often as life permits: I sometimes wonder, as we soar exuberantly over a fence, if I would have hated horses had they been part of the school curriculum. My working life is spent watching sport, talking to athletes, and it is great.

When I hear about the decline in sports at schools because of lack of funds, or because of the increasingly popular notion that competitive games are bad vibes, my feelings are very mixed. School games always seemed to be for the few people who were awfully good at them, just as English lessons seemed to be for the people who were good at things like discussing *Finnegans Wake* and *The Rainbow*.

I don't know if the people who miss out discover the pleasure of great writing later in life: it would be nice to think so. Certainly sport's pleasures came to me long after I had drunk my last half of Starlight, and when they came, they were far more intoxicating. But the thing is, when I hear about the woes of school games, I always think, not about the England players who are lost to us as a school gives up rugby, but of the hundreds and thousands of miserable Wednesday afternoons that the enormous majority of the pupils have endured – and from which they will now be saved.

I have always rather admired Mike Gatting for his refusal to take failure for an answer. No one had more last chances than him, no one looked more oppressed and harried a Test player. That he succeeded in becoming England captain and England's most danger-ous batsman is a tribute to the stubbornness that is a vital part of his make-up. This piece was basically a piece of speculation: the one thing I am certain of is that if Gatt was asked if I was right, he would deny it. Sportsmen always deny things like that. Mental weakness? Never heard of the stuff!

SWEEPING REVERSAL OF ROLES FOR 'UNCOOL' GATTING
June 1987

And so Good Ol' Gatt has got an OBE. He celebrated by hitting 196 at the weekend, reaching his ton with a reverse sweep: the shot that made him the man he is today. Perhaps the shot that set him on course for the gong. For it was with a reverse sweep that he publicly out-cooled Botham and showed the audience of millions that at last he was every bit as much an international cricketer as the Golden Boy.

For years, Gatting had been a bit of an outsider in England cricket. He had never collected the results, had never been a regular. He had never been accepted as an international cricketer, not by the selectors, not by the public, and not by the clique at the heart of the team.

His most memorable act had been to get himself out lbw without playing a stroke twice in the same Test match, and it gave him a dreadful mental wound. 'I don't get out like that in county matches,' he said at the time. 'Everything is tuned higher in Test cricket, but that is not why I have failed. The failures were of my own making.'[1] But it was never Gatting's talent that was in doubt. That he has not ceased from mental fight is a triumph worthy of a medal.

He had always felt intimidated by Botham: even more than most cricketers. They both set out to make their names together in 1977 in Pakistan and New Zealand. Botham scored a century and deliberately ran out Boycott: there can be few better ways of making friends. His marvellous international career had begun. Gatting was overshadowed completely, and his in-and-out Test career had started. Every time he looked over his shoulder Botham was out there performing miracles for England.

When Gatting was included in the Test side, he was not one of the cool guys, but outside the in-crowd. One can sometimes forget that prodigious sportsmen often have minds and motivations as small as those of ordinary chaps. Botham loves in-crowds: and any clique is defined by exclusion. Botham, Willis, Gower, Lamb: it was they who counted in the team.

Gatting would probably have been counted out of Test cricket without the generous mind and perceptive qualities of Gower: he wanted Gatting as his vice-captain in India. Botham, you will recall, did not tour: Gatt blossomed. He started scoring Test centuries. The only doubt that remained was whether he could do it back home, with Botham alongside.

So then came the day of the reverse sweep: the shot, you will remember, had been adopted by Botham as one of his trademarks: like the Rasta wristband and the hammy bat-whirling entrance. Gatting and Botham both played in the first one-dayer in 1985 against Australia. Botham was going brilliantly, looking set for a ton or better.

Gatting came out to join him, and almost at once had the colossal effrontery to play the reverse sweep, and to good effect. Botham was inevitably goaded beyond endurance by this challenge – and from such a source – to his majesty. He promptly played the reverse sweep himself and missed. He was bowled for 72, totally out-cooled, and because of it, England lost the match.

But Gatting had won something of vast significance to himself. He had taunted Botham and won. He had no further need to prove himself to the in-crowd. He was vice-captain, an established batsman, and soon enough he became captain. Now he has led England through a memorable winter in Australia.

He is mentally tough because he has had to labour and sweat and despair to earn every moment of triumph. There is no doubt now that Gatting is in charge. The sloppy in-group mentality, something some observers see as a hangover from those weird triumphs of 1981, is no more. I wonder how much of his personal triumph Gatting puts down to that enormous private victory in the duel of the reverse sweeps two summers ago.

[1] Note this quote lifted from my series on the yips (see page 47).

I didn't expect to like Las Vegas, but I had always wanted to go and see what it was really like. For some extraordinary reason, it has a reputation for being a glamorous place. I thought it was the least glamorous place in the world; at least, I did until I went to Atlantic City. The only thing I liked was the Circus Circus, which is so horribly bizarre, so utterly surreal, that I kept going back there. It helped me get the town into perspective. The reason for the trip, by the way, was to watch Tony Tucker spend 10 rounds keeping out of Mike Tyson's way.

TYSON TAKES A BACK SEAT TO TUXEDO-CLAD HIGH ROLLERS
August 1987

Las Vegas: If you ever go to watch a world championship fight in Las Vegas and you want to get the whole thing in perspective, make a visit to Circus Circus. There you can play

146

the tables and the slots while above your head, circus acts are performed from 11 a.m. till midnight: the Flying Cavaretas, Anna's Russian Wolfhounds, Los Armandos Motorcycle Aerial Ballet, and more, and more.

All around is a kind of gambler's kindergarten: throw a hoop and win a four-foot-high polar bear; flick a mock chicken carcass into a cooking pot and win a neon-green dinosaur. Children run everywhere clutching paper cups full of dollar bills. Hunter S. Thompson wrote about the place in his masterwork, *Fear And Loathing in Las Vegas*: 'The Circus Circus is what the whole hep world would be doing on Saturday night if the Nazis had won the war.'

But only if there were no fight in town. I met a man in the lift (or elevator) who was flying out high rollers from the East Coast to watch the fight. They would get a $750 ticket, free rooms, free drink, even food – if they wanted such a peculiar thing. 'I guess they'll each play for about four hours a day, minimum. For $100 a hand. I guess they'll all win or lose $10,000. Minimum.'

Or, to put it another way, lose. That is why they have boxing in Las Vegas: never mind that they took more than $2 million on the gate. The real point is that a fight brings the high rollers into town. As one of the hotel fight managers said: 'I think certain big names don't draw gamblers. For instance, Frank Sinatra draws a big gambling crowd, whereas someone like Willie Nelson won't.' But a heavyweight world championship fight will always bring the gamblers, along with the pimps, the hookers, the jailbirds, the con-artists, the hangers-on, and all the tuxedo-clad aristocracy you associate with the noble art of boxing. And for all these men with the bulging money clips, boxing is just one more ring in the 24-hour Circus Circus.

Win a polar bear! Watch two black men thump each other's brains out! It is all part of the eternal background to the playing of moronic games for mind-buckling sums of money. Mike Tyson may have been crowned with a plastic crown, and a fake ermine robe wrapped about him, after he beat Tony Tucker on Saturday night to become the undisputed heavyweight champion of the world, but as the phoney ceremony went on, the real action of the night continued at the tables.

You might arrive here, jet-lagged, at midnight and watch people gambling as you check into your hotel. You can get up at six and go down for breakfast: the same gamblers will still be there. You can reach for the phone: 'Over 20 of the most beautiful and sexiest XXX-rated nude dancers and exotic nude strippers are available to you 24-hours-a-day, *direct to your room*. Major credit cards accepted.'

The point is that boxers are no more than triple X-rated bodies themselves. Indeed, Tucker only owns 50 per cent of himself. It is estimated that all he will end up taking away from this fight will be $90,000. But Tyson, some believe, could end up earning more money in the ring than Muhammad Ali: he already has $25 million in prize money, and that is over a third of the way there. And at only 21 years of age.

But there remains a kind of innocence about these fighting men. They are awesome athletes, men who believe they are doing right. It is the men behind them, the fixers, the managers, the bullies, the promoters, the hangers-on, the men who are responsible for the entire Circus Circus of the 'sport', that are such a loathsome bunch.

Here is a neurological note: anyone who suffers from concussion cannot but end up with permanent brain damage, ergo the principle of boxing is to cause permanent brain damage in your opponent. On my good days, I believe that in the not-too-distant future it will seem incredible that boxing had existed.

The trouble is, I do not have very many good days in Las Vegas. The circus goes on 24 hours a day: trapeze artists, Frank Sinatra, Mike Tyson in a plastic crown, the orang-utan act, the polar bear game, Mike Tyson damaging brains. 'No,' wrote Hunter S. Thompson, 'this is not a good town for psychedelic drugs. Reality itself is too twisted.'

From the Diary

My first England goat team – I borrow the term from America – comes from Alan Kirby, who gets a *Times* tenner for his researches. He has relied entirely on statistical evidence for his no-hopers XI. Three matches for England is his qualification: 'It is easy to demonstrate incompetence in one or two games, but proving it requires three.' Here is the team: batting average is followed, where appropriate, by bowling average.

1 Hon. Ivo Bligh, 10.3
2 D. V. Smith, 8.3
3 G. D. Barlow, 4.25
4 Lord Hawke, 7.9
5 E. G. Hayes, 10.75
6 G. B. Studd, 4.4
7 J. H. Board, 10.8
8 H. Howell, 7.5, 79.9
9 M. W. W. Selvey, 7.2, 57.2
10 M. F. Tremlett, 6.7, 56.5
11 T. B. Mitchell, 5.0, 62.25

Mr Kirby said that if everyone batted his average, the total without extras would be 87, while the bowlers would concede around 600. He adds a rider that Lord Hawke could not necessarily be trusted to lead the team to defeat, since he actually won two matches in South Africa. But in those matches he scored a total of nine runs and did not bowl, so is selected on personal performance. There are wicket-keepers with worse batting averages than Board, but no one can rival his 11 victims in 12 innings. Incidentally, the list includes some terrific county players, and let me add that M. W. W. Selvey is now a terrific writer as well, so he needn't throw things at me in the Press box next season.

> This was a Botham rides off into the sunset piece, a premature obituary. National hero, national pain-in-the-arse, but still the most important cricketer of the age.

TIME TO TAKE STOCK OF BOTHAM
August 1987

'Go on, Ian,' they cried yesterday as Botham strode out to the middle. What? Did they really believe that Botham was about to score a breezy 700 and then bounce out the opposition for an encore? Perhaps they did. Certainly they believed that if anyone could do such things it was Botham.

Today is the last day of the last Test match of the summer. In the winter Botham will be an Australian,[1] something he does increasingly well. England's Test matches in Pakistan and New Zealand will go on without him. And so, perhaps, today will be the last day of Botham's Test career. Who can say?

It all feels rather like the end of an era. Certainly this match had a *fin de siècle* air about it. Somewhere in the middle of it Botham scored his 5,000th Test run, among which he has scored 14 centuries. He has taken 373 Test wickets and 109 catches. It is surely the most remarkable set of figures in the history of international cricket.

I think we are all rather too close to him and rather too close to his years of – comparative – decline to come to terms with his full greatness. Also, we are too close to all the silly bits: his outbreaks of twittishness, the scandals, the publicity machine, his bizarre relationship with popular newspapers and the rest. Furthermore, in our short-term memories his days of disappointment are more vivid: the long hops, the flailing-bat dismissals, the temperamental outbursts.

All the same, Botham is the most important cricketer of our age. Is it an over-assessment to say that Botham is England's most significant cricketer since W.G. Grace? Grace was the man who founded the modern era of cricket: the colossus, the enormous personality, the first true sporting star, the man for whom they put up the prices when he came in to bat, a Bothamesque touch, if ever there was one.

Botham in his turn became the spearhead, if you like, of the post-modern era. Cricket has become a global circus of international matches. It needs high-profile personalities. A broad popular appeal is essential to keep the wheels of the juggernaut turning. Botham became the central personality in cricket's new age of the television camera and the jumbo jet. If Grace was cricket's first star, Botham was its first superstar.

His career falls neatly into The Three Ages of Both, each signified by alterations in his appearance, doubtless consciously assumed. He began as The Tousle-Haired Kid, first coming to attention in a one-day match for Somerset. He was hit in the face by an Andy Roberts bouncer, spat two teeth on to the pitch and scored a match-winning 45. He became a Test player and after 19 matches had taken 100 wickets. After 21 he had 1,000 runs. It's all come too early, everyone said. He'll never know such times again.

But then came the era of The Bearded Lion. One prodigious feat followed another, briefly interrupted by that sad period as England captain. After the captaincy came the Year of the Three Miracles: 1981 and all that. The three Tests he won against Australia will still defy belief when people watch the videos in the 21st century.

But this staggering overachievement ushered in the next change of identity: The Golden-Haired Film Star. By this time Botham had become the most famous sportsman in Britain, a remarkable thing for a cricketer. Indeed, his became the most recognisable face in the country outside the Royal Family.

What George Best did for football Botham did for cricket. Each made his game the biggest news in the land. And, of course, the coin has a reverse[2] side. You are rich and famous beyond your dreams: but you have had to become public property. And if you do anything wrong you are likely to get found out and exposed with unseemly delight. His finger-clickin' former agent, Tim Hudson, called Botham 'The World's First Rock 'n' Roll Cricketer'. Botham also managed to become the world's first sex 'n' drugs cricketer. Inevitably, he went to Hollywood to try to be a film star.

The weight of his personal mythology was enormous. No one could produce performances to justify his kind of legendary status, not every day. And so the criticism became both regular and perverse. The man once praised for his attacking bowling was hammered for not bowling with line and length. The man once praised for his devil-may-care batting was castigated for his recklessness. And most of the criticism has come because Test matches do sometimes go by without his scoring 149 or 118 or taking five for one. Time and again he has confounded the critics; time and again he has played into their hands.

Botham has frequently said that his prime irritation with cricket is that 'too many people live in the past.' But Botham himself is destined to become one of those great lumbering figures of cricketing legend. And as we speak reverently of his achievements, as we certainly will in 20 years or so, we will irritate thoroughly every young thruster out to make a name for himself in the modern game.

'But the modern game is what it is today because of Botham,' they will be told. 'Ah, shut up. Pass me my blue flannels, my 5 lb bat and the hairbrush. The cameras are turning *now*.' And for 20 years the cameras, the spectators and the selectors will have been looking for a new Botham. And they still won't have found him.

---

[1] Of course, he got chucked out of Australian cricket after putting a fellow airline passenger in a headlock. 'He just happened to be on the wrong plane at the wrong time,' said Botham. The Australian attitude of primness and hypocrisy to all this was a collector's item: the country that had idolised the boorishness of Lillee and the Chappells got up on its high horse and said Botham was too rough for them.

[2] Not an obverse side, if I may be excused a burst of pedantry. The obverse is the main face of the coin, 'heads' if you prefer. Tails is the reverse side.

I went out to cover the World Series in October. There I was, an Englishman lost in the middle of America, the kind of America nobody knows about, Minneapolis and St Louis, up at the wrong end of the Mississippi, and following a uniquely and quintessentially American sport. It was a wonderful trip. Here follow the first and the last pieces of the Series.

A GRAND SLAM HOMER OF A NIGHT
October 1987

Minnesota is not a state that goes in for big emotion. Someone once said a typical Minnesota conversation went like this:
'What d'ya think of the weather?'
'Boy, it's something.'
'I've never seen anything like it.'
'You've got that right.'
You leave the volatile reactions to the strange people who live on the coasts, right? You bet. (The last is a crucial phrase here, I am told. Use it for everything.)

But on Saturday night Minneapolis went off its head. Drivers honked their horns unceasingly, people just couldn't stop making those gibbon-like whooping calls that Americans go in for on sporting occasions, and pedestrians ran in and out of the traffic exchanging high-fives with ecstatic car passengers hanging perilously out of the windows. And it went on for hours; the town was in the grip of sheer unbridled delight. The place had gone mad and fallen utterly in love with itself. Why not? The Minnesota Twins had won a baseball game. They beat the St Louis Cardinals 10-1 in the first game in the World Series, a baseball competition that America always wins. In the best-of-seven series, Minnesota had struck the first blow.

There was not a building, not a bank, not a shop that did not display its 'Win Twins' slogans – Minnesota Twins named for, if you will pardon the vernacular, the twin cities of Minneapolis and St Paul, cities which sit either side of the Mississippi – though not Huck Finn's Mississippi; we are in the far north up here.

Minnesota is not a place accustomed to success. Schulz, the man who gave us Peanuts, had his cartoons rejected from the high school yearbook when he was at school in St Paul. The Twins haven't won anything since 1965, when they won the American League but lost the World Series.

So going over the top can be excused a little, for once. The noise level in the Hubert H. Humphrey Metrodome – named for the late Vice-President – reached a peak of 118 decibels when Dan Gladden hit a grand slam homer. That is as loud as a jet plane taking off. A grand slam homer, by the way, is a home run with a runner on every base, which is therefore worth four runs: rather as if a cricketer hit a six and was credited with about 250 runs. It was the first grand slam homer in the World Series since 1970; something worth shouting for. They almost raised the roof.

Yes, roof. The Metrodome is an indoor stadium, and this is the first time the World Series has been played in one. They play two games here, then the next three in St Louis, under God's own roof. Then, if necessary, we are back in the Metrodome for games six and seven. Home advantage might just be critical.[1]

And the Metrodome is a quirky place, even without the noise and the waving of 'Homer Hankies'. The Twins have established the best home record in the American League this season, and are now on a roll, as they say, hammering the League's 'winningest team', the Detroit Tigers, in the play-offs and winning triumphantly on Saturday.

It was an hour and 10 minutes before the Twins managed their first hit. After another 18 minutes and another five hits, the score had advanced to 7-1 in a monstrous fourth inning that lifted the hearts of the neutrals and drove the Minnesotans out of their collective tree.

It left the Cardinals cursing the Metrodome, as so many other teams have before. They called it 'the Homerdome' when it first opened in 1982, because of the regularity with

154

which balls flew over the fence. The introduction of air conditioning has changed that a little – the stadium was only eighth of the Major League stadiums in home runs total this season. But visiting teams still hate it. They lose fly balls in the roof, the noise is horrible, and they hardly ever win. The journos now call it 'the Metrodoom'.

Another archetypal Minnesotan remark: 'I tried one game in there. I don't remember who was playing centre field. But it made me dizzy and a little sick to my stomach to see that far and still be inside a building.' It is 408 feet from home plate to the fence at centre field, so it is understandable. But on Saturday night no one was about to criticise it, not in Minneapolis. Yup, they even call it Dome Sweet Dome. You bet.

VIOLA PLAYS THE SWEETEST MUSIC IN ALL MINNESOTA
October 1987

It was a uniquely American celebration. They didn't actually dance in the streets of Minneapolis but they had an incredibly jolly traffic jam. Every hooter in the city was blaring, people hung out of the car windows, loonies ran round in the traffic high-fiving everyone they could see; and they didn't get tired of it for hours.

The match ended at 10.30; at one in the morning the celebrations were still going on: with a Poop-poop! Twins! No 1, yeah! The Lord of Misrule had taken over, people climbed up the traffic lights, bounced on car bonnets, rode on the roofs of buses, clambered on to shop awnings. The entire town was caught up in ecstasies of delight and the people who ran the restaurant I was in gave me a lift to my hotel because there was not a taxi to be had for love nor money.[2]

What Hubert Humphrey couldn't do, what Walter Mondale couldn't do, was finally done by a bunch of baseball players that no one had given a chance to. Minnesota is not a state that wins things: it tends to come puffing up in second place, but not too worried, because it was what they had expected all along.

This is the state that shrugs and says: 'Whatever.' This is a classic Minnesota expression and it implies a stance of philosophical resignation: 'I'm going to have to replace all the wiring. It ain't going to be cheap.' 'Whatever.' They are very good at fishing in all the lakes around here and are much better than New Yorkers at catching wall-eyed pike. But winning big ball games? It never happens here.

But on Sunday, in a game of white-knuckle baseball, Minnesota Twins won the final game of the World Series for a victory over the St Louis Cardinals by four games to three and, on the night, by a stomach-churning four runs to two. It was not a night of exuberant hitting: it was a night of scrambling and hoping and praying that the arm and the nerve of the pitcher held good.

The pitcher for the Twins was Frankie 'Sweet Music' Viola. He had joined the Twins five years ago, the year that a band of the Twins stalwarts came into the side: Hrbek, Gaetti, Brunansky, Laudener and Bush: the Class of '82. In their first season they lost 102 games, the most the club had lost since moving from Washington in 1961.

But they improved. The following season they lost only 92 games. They improved again in 1984, coming second in the west division, and then went backwards again, losing 176 games in two seasons. This is the Twins they're used to here: that is why the celebrations were so long, so incredulous and so quaintly innocent.

Viola was a pretty talented pitcher when he joined the club but no good in a crisis. When things got sticky Viola got rattled and if there is one thing that batters love it is a rattled pitcher. That is why pitchers become such grim and forbidding men: 'When things went wrong, I'd show my emotions,' Viola said. 'That would hurt both me and my team mates.'

In the second inning of the crucial game on Sunday night Viola went wrong again: he conceded four hits from which the Cardinals scampered in two runs. Once again the Twins looked a beaten side. But throughout the next six innings Viola was a man possessed. No one could lay bat on ball: he conceded just two hits in those innings and no runs at all.

156

As the Twins struggled and lurched to a 3-2 lead Viola kept hammering the ball in over the plate. In the end he was given the series' Most Valuable Player award for his near-perfect pitching in games one and seven, his defeat in St Louis being set aside. 'Incredible,' he said. 'We've come so far since 1982 it's unbelievable.' Being a sucker for the underdogs can be hard going. It means you back a lot of slow horses, cheer for a lot of losers, seek in vain for the spirit of Pak Doo Ik in every band of no-hopers. Whatever.

No one had really believed in their hearts that the Twins could manage this win: hence the insane celebrations. Go to New York for some peace and quiet and sanity. Minneapolis is off its bonce. When the final out was recorded on Sunday night the decibel meter hit 120 and those who were silent were either men of iron or of St Louis. It was one of the great emotional occasions of sport.

[1] It was. Every game in the series was won by the home side, the first time this had ever happened.
[2] Use of this fact meant that it would have been unstylish to claim $20 on expenses for the cab I would have taken.

I do not normally go in for action-man reporting. But here was a challenge I had no intention of resisting. Well, not a challenge but a temptation, and I can resist anything except temptation.

A COMMONER AT THE SPORT OF PRINCES
November 1987

Faithful readers of this space would have noticed that something of my habitual iron restraint goes out the window when I come to write about the horsy sports. One person who noticed this was Douglas Brown. Brown is one of those no-nonsense, devastatingly straightforward chaps. He plays, of all things, polo. He took it up late in life and thinks it is just about the best sport in the world.

In his no-nonsense way he gets tremendously sick of reading about polo in magazines. All princes and flowing frocks and Jeremy Hyphen-Hyphen-Money enjoying a joke with the Hon Arabella. Polo is not seen as a sport any more: is an image used to sell just about anything that costs a great deal more than it ought to.

The popular notion of the game itself is as a kind of marbles played on very tame animals. Brown, chairman of Cirencester Polo Club, challenged me to play the game myself and tell the world the truth. With no help at all from the Hon Arabella. And so, with my best riding boots in my bag and not a little trepidation in my heart, I went to Cheltenham to meet Nicky Williams. Williams buys, trains or 'makes' and sells polo ponies, schools polo ponies and players and also plays like a demon for Cirencester.

He put me on one of his ponies and started telling me what to do. It was one of the most disorientating experiences you could wish for. Imagine jumping into a car and finding all the controls, including the steering wheel, in the wrong place. And to make things more interesting, all the controls are about three times more sensitive than you expect: oversteer, overcorrect, a light touch on the brakes and you are halfway up your pony's neck.

There are many terrible myths about polo ponies: horse people always have awful stories about the heartlessness of people in different parts of the horsy world. The theory is that polo ponies have mouths like icebreakers and are worked so hard they are clapped out years before their time. Well, I rode a slip of a thing of 19, as fizzy and as jolly a chap as you could wish for and yet who stopped at the merest nudge on the reins. All the ponies I rode were beauties and a retired polo pony would make the most splendid hack. (Believe me, I know a lot about hacks.)

I first learned to ride for dressage, show jumping and cross-country. This was all different. It is no part of dressage to canter straight at the wall and whizz back at a full canter with scarcely a break in stride. With but a single hand on the reins – obviously you need a spare hand for the stick – the horse responds to the rein pressure on the neck and is supernaturally responsive to shifts of weight in the saddle: you lean the way you want to go. A useful by-product of this is that the horse will naturally tend to try to catch you if you slip.

It is all about sitting deep in the saddle, like a dressage rider, but instead of performing calm, precise movements you perform wild and excited precise movements. Polo ponies are a wonderful new world of horsemanship. The ultimate aim of your own and the horse's schooling is to control the pony with no more conscious thought than you use to control your own legs in football. For the ball is the thing. The trouble is, you move as fast as an ice hockey player but aim to strike the ball from a moving platform and with a stick all but five feet long. It is, as you can imagine, quite fiendishly difficult.

Williams and Brown next had me doing 'stick and ball' at Cirencester, which was good fun. It involves cantering about the place trying to whack a ridiculously tiny ball with your ridiculously long stick. By the time both pony and I had a serious sweat on I was beginning to get the hang of it. Sort of. Williams told me afterwards that my riding was better than my rather approximate stuff with the stick. It was a wrench to be less than perfect but at least it was the right way round to get it wrong, I felt.

Williams and Brown were determined to complete my polo education and so they told me that the thing to do was to play in a few practice chukkas. I turned chicken and said I'd be totally out of my depth but they were inexorable. I wanted to see what it was like, didn't I?

I played in a three-a-side practice match at Williams' tufty and undulating polo field. One of my opponents bounced the ball on the end of his stick half a dozen times in an awesomely casual sort of way. He, inevitably, was the man I had to mark – that and score the goals. 'You are the spearhead,' I was told. How good an idea was that?

And then on into the heat and chaos of the game. Galloping like fury in all directions, ball-chasing like a tyro footballer, chasing back to mark this young superstar who hit the ball several hundred yards with every blow. 'Ride him off, ride him off,' they shouted at me.

It was when I discovered that this is not a game for gentlemen that I began to enjoy myself. When your superstar is chasing the ball it is your duty to assault him a little. You can hook his stick with your own or, better still, bundle into him, horse, legs, elbows, shoulders and anything else handy. This is, I learned rapidly and to my surprise, a game of fierce physical contact. At 40 mph and at a nice, bone-breaking height above the ground.

In the second chukka I switched to a muscly, confident and pugnacious scrapper of a horse who loved to get in there and shove. He suited my mood to perfection: if I couldn't show any skill, at least I was going to get stuck in and mess a few people about. And as I brought the ethics of football rather than croquet into play I was able to harry and chase with occasional flashes of purpose.

I hit the ball, I think, a total of twice in three chukkas. Once I backhanded to one of my own players, which was something of a surprise. The other time I smote the ground a mighty blow, damn near broke my wrist, shoved the ball about two feet and galloped over it, overshooting by yards. I clean missed an open goal when a six-inch tap was required. Only connect, as E.M. Forster said.

I finished hot, sweaty and pugnacious. This is a game of confrontation, hot-blooded involvement and terrible language. It is a game for getting stuck in and going like a rocket. It is a game of great skill and a touch of savagery. It is about getting covered in horse sweat and human sweat and, more than anything else, it is about horses and horsemanship. It is bloody marvellous fun.

> This was a bizarre trip: going to Rome with football writers to look at non-representational art. One of my colleagues roared with laughter and asked what it could 'mean'; another, a renaissance man and a painter's son, took a different attitude. It provided material for another piece about the arties and the hearties, indeed, enough material to have made me shut up on the subject ever since.

BLACK IS BEAUTIFUL FOR WORLD CUP
November 1987

So let's bring together a bunch of football writers from all over Europe and give them a treat, all right? Let's put them on a train in Rome, unship them in Umbria, and show them round an art gallery. And let's show them something they can get their teeth into: some difficult and challenging non-representational art. Yes, let's give them Alberto Burri: the man who uses torn sackcloth, burnt and ripped plastic and cracked ceramics. That will give them a nice change from writing about groin strains.

So that is exactly what the organisers of the 1990 World Cup did. The competition will be held in Italy: it seems that art and sport have a different relationship over there. The English World Cup poster for 1966 had all the commitment and thought you would expect from an advertising agency. It showed a lion dressed as a footballer.

Other nations have had more elevated ideas: poster designers of the past include Miró and Dali. And the Italians asked Burri to do the poster for Italia 90: Burri of the paintings that come in three shades of black as the only colour, Burri of the tortured hessian and brutalised Cellotex.

Well, we saw what Burri has come up with. Curious lighting on the Colosseum: well, no, actually. Burri has used a negative. The black image dominates all the posters: colour is only used on the football pitch in the centre. I think it is a cracker, myself, and so do the World Cup people. Burri must be pretty pleased with it himself: he is, I am told, a bit of a football fan. Well, what is so funny about an artist who likes to watch the lads at weekends?

Many great men have also been football enthusiasts: I have a small but choice collection of the names of great men who have played at goalkeeper: Albert Camus, Vladimir Nabokov, Yevgeny Yevtushenko, and, naturally, the Pope. But you will notice that these people are all Europeans. The Italians thought it quite reasonable to take football writers to check out a bit of non-representational art: it seems to be only in Britain that art and sport are mutually exclusive. The sportsman's knee-jerk philistinism is a strictly British phenomenon.

I suspect it all goes back to Rugby School and its spirit of manly philistinism: its equation, if you like, of manliness *with* philistinism. This has been followed, inevitably and much less excusably, by the intellectuals' total rejection of sport. To be completely uninterested in sport of every kind is seen as the hallmark of a member of the intelligentsia. It is philistinism in another coat.

The sporting man's notion of Intellectual Man is of Anthony Blanche in *Brideshead Revisited*: he summed up the eternal divide between the arties and hearties when he read *The Wasteland* through a loud hailer to passing oarsmen. It was the hearties' ambition to duck him in a fountain: 'You can't think how much pleasure it would give me to be manhandled by you meaty boys.' To the sporting man, Blanche *is* art: posing, vain, effete, unnatural, prompting fear and loathing.

And to the arties, sport is the pursuit of the small-brained man, the unworthy, the brutal, the insensitive, the unaware, the man of wide eyes and closed mind. Let us take a look at the *London Review of Books*, which recently carried a piece about Hans Keller, the music critic. '... the image comes to mind when I think of Hans and football and my inability to say anything about it at all ... I confess to conceiving a gross disproportion between the skilled attention Hans gave soccer and the skills the game brings into play. Why didn't Hans grow out of this surely adolescent enthusiasm?'

But this drew a spirited reply in the letters column from

Robert Stewart, from which I quote: 'Of sport three defences (it should need no defence!) may briefly be made: 1, It asks of the species, purely and with no ulterior end, that it should test its limits ...; 2, It reminds us, with grace and passion, that life itself is a game ... again to be played gloriously (as Hans Keller played it) according to the rules down to the final whistle; 3, It reveals to us that one of life's chief pleasures, perhaps the chief pleasure of all, is to draw out the best in others ...

'Does (the writer) think that Neville Cardus' love of cricket was adolescent? Might he not pause to ask himself why it is that football drew from Keller and cricket from Cardus such excellent prose? He could begin in the knowledge of A.J. Ayer's love of football and G.H. Hardy's love of cricket, by considering what music, philosophy, mathematics and sport have in common: namely that each is a useless, exhilarating *abstraction*.'

It is ridiculous that something as basically jolly as sport needs to be justified to some people: it is ridiculous that sport inspired so much contempt in the first place. But then the hearties' hatred and suspicion of anything remotely arty is every bit as absurd. Those who inhabit either side of this great rift valley are the poorer for it.

I am on the side of the renaissance man myself: those who can see nobility in all forms of pure endeavour and ugliness in every form of cheating: those who can enjoy goals, symphonies, runs, wickets, poems and paintings made of sackcloth. Let Blanche scull along the river while the college eight chants *The Waste Land* to him: 'You! *Hypocrite lecteur! – mon semblable – mon frère!*'

This is a piece included for historical reasons. It was my reaction to the great Shakhoor Rana/Mike Gatting umpiring rumpus, and it got me a great sackful of hate mail. So I think it must have touched the odd nerve.

CRICKET'S WILD COLONIAL BOYS
December 1987

The current cricket-spawned crisis is being compared to the Bodyline Series. This is a good comparison. The villain of the piece, the Australians believe, was not Larwood, who bowled so fiercely, but his captain, Jardine. Jardine embodied all the instinctive colonial arrogance that Australians hate more than anything in the world.

It happens that the Pakistanis hate it just as much. And it is colonial arrogance, or at least a throw back to it, that is the heart of the matter now. Consider how the Pakistanis see this crisis. Cricket is, politically, a game about the abandonment of empire and the ambitions of former colonies. And if you look at the situation from the point of view of the former colony, you see England acting with all the traditional arrogance of masters.

England might have had a strong moral position in all this mess but they have blown it completely. There have been umpiring problems in Test matches between England and Pakistan as long as the nations have played cricket together. The problem, in English eyes, is that Pakistani umpires cheat and Pakistani players whinge when rightly given out by English umpires, who are, naturally, 'the best in the world.'

The Pakistanis do not see it in quite the same way. They have found some English umpiring genuinely unsatisfactory. They agreed that umpiring was a problem and wanted to have neutral umpires for the series last summer in England. Oh, no, English umpires are the best in the world, imagine what neutral umpires would lead to, why, you would end up with little brown chaps umpiring Ashes matches!

The Pakistanis then requested, as was their right, that David Constant, an umpire who had got up their noses in the past, be replaced. Replace him? My dear little brown chaps, he is an English umpire and that means he is one of the best umpires in the world! It is not surprising that the Pakistanis were extremely annoyed at cricket's bland colonial arrogance. But it seems to have surprised everybody in English cricket, all the same.

Last summer's matches were concluded in acrimony. The Pakistani tour manager was portrayed everywhere as a figure of fun and one of the papers ran a story headlined, as I recall, 'Ten Ways the Pakistanis Cheat Our Boys.'[1]

With all this as a background, plus Pakistan's poor showing in the World Cup, the first Test of the present series was set up for heightened emotion. And the umpiring was so absolutely appalling and became so big an issue that it seemed inevitable that something would be done about it at last.

But England blew it. By open dissent, and by implicit support of open dissent from captain and tour management, England abandoned the principles of fair play they claimed they were defending. In effect, they said that if a Pakistani refuses to walk, it is because he is a cheat; when an Englishman refuses to walk, it is because the umpire is a cheat. In the immortal words of Mike Gatting: 'One rule for them, one for us.'

And so, obsessed by their one-eyed vision of wrong-doings, by some genuine injustices, by xenophobia, by injured innocence, the England cricket party have retreated into a laager. The unbelievable, small-mindedness of Gatting's refusal to apologise to the umpire 'unless the umpire apologises for what he has said' pushed the row from a sporting squabble into an international incident.[2]

I dare say the umpire was in the wrong but, with Gatting's rant, he and England have forfeited all claim to moral rightness. Gatting was much provoked, I am sure: that is a good reason for what he did but it is no excuse. The issue should have been about the dreadful umpiring. But England have got it so completely wrong that the row is not about that at all now. It is about England's open defiance of the rules and tradition of the game.

---

[1] Most of these were the daily bread of county cricket.
[2] It was Gatting's stubbornness that gave him the resilience to become an international cricketer of stature, as related on page 144. This was the reverse (yes, reverse) side of the coin.

Here are some further reflections after the Shakhoor
Rana incident. This was illustrated with mug-shots of all
the England captains from Denness to Gatting. After
the summer of 1988, there would not have been room
for my own thoughts if all the captains were included. I
think I can claim this piece as an accurate prophecy.

A TOUR THROUGH THE MINEFIELD OF CAPTAINCY
December 1987

My mother always wanted me to be Prime Minister by the
time I was 24. I would rush to the House to save the nation,
still in my flannels after scoring a century as England captain
at Lord's. Thank God, I have fallen short of her hopes. I
would have had problems with the ethics as a politician (mine,
I mean) while being England cricket captain is, I think, the
most impossibly demanding job in the world.

In the last dozen years it is hard to think of a man whom the
captaincy has not somehow diminished. Four of the six men
appointed as captain before Gatting were actually fired
(though, to be pedantic, Botham resigned about half an inch
ahead of the boot). Fletcher, regarded as the finest captain in
county cricket, was fired. Greig, grovelling before the altar of
money, was fired. Gower won from one-down in India, won
the Ashes and was fired.

Willis was a much-loved figure when he was made captain:
when he retired from the job he was a figure of fun,
caricatured as the moron at mid-on. Boycott, who had four
Tests as stand-in captain, was deliberately run out by a young
thruster called Botham and then sat for hours with his head
in a towel.

'What about Brearley?' I hear you say. 'Surely he was the
one man who came out of the captaincy with his reputation
enhanced?' He did but it took a miracle or two to do it,

166

specifically the miracles of 1981. Before that, he had been much criticised, not for his captaincy but for his batting. 'There were 50 better batsmen in England,' Boycott said, unkindly.

Being England captain is not just the most thankless job in sport; it is also the most demanding. There is no team sport in which so much depends on one man's constant decision-making. The game spins around the two captains: the pace and the nature of the contest come from them.

Bobby Robson has a tough job but at least he doesn't have to play as well. England's cricket captain must make the crucial decisions and also get his own game together. Not easy. Gatting is criticised for sweeping all before him;[1] poor Denness went to the length of dropping himself; Brearley's form was intermittent; the captaincy drastically affected Botham's form; Gower felt that troughs in form affected his decision-making.

These pressures are tough enough. But that is only the cricket half of the job: there is a lot more to being England captain. This is because of the nature of the game. There is a portentousness about cricket that all other games lack.[2] Say a bunch of players get drunk and smash up a hotel room. (It has been known, after all.) If they are rugby players, they are good ol' boys. If they are footballers, they are unsavoury yobs. If they are cricketers, it is an international scandal.

The England captain is also the Press spokesman, which is about as jolly a job as skipping through a minefield. Botham likes to be seen as a bluff, ornery sort of chap but in one area he became as morbidly sensitive as Marcel Proust: personal criticism. Willis' dislike of the Press became a burning obsession. 'I rather enjoyed it,' Brearley said. 'I felt it was a kind of game in which you had to be careful not to step off the wall.' But captains less light on their feet verbally have had hard times.

England captains are peculiarly vulnerable to criticism. Every setback can look like the captain's fault. For some reason, it is considered that putting your opponent in is a reckless gamble and if an insertion fails to result in bowling the opposition out for 120 then the captain has bungled.

Hence the unfairest sporting headline of the year: 'Gatt the Prat.'

But still we are not through with the job's responsibilities. What other job makes such diplomatic demands? Cricket is, in all Test-playing nations, a special thing, and the demands of a touring captain are immense. And tours give you three months in the limelight, not 90 minutes. History is full of England captains who have blown it diplomatically. Greig did it in a single word;[3] Jardine took longer but was more comprehensive; Fletcher blew it in his dog-in-the-manger tour of India, which became a slow over-rate competition; and Gatting, I fear, has also blown it.

Gower had to deal with the problems after two political assassinations in India and then with the death-threats and demonstrations in Trinidad. He was fired for his lack of bustle: we see now where Gatting's wholeheartedness has got us. An England captain cannot win.

'You are carrying all the prejudices of England,' Brearley said. 'You are representing deep and paranoid urges jingoistic sentiments you may prefer to distance yourself from. But it is unavoidable.' All England captains are forced to bear the burden of national machismo in their hands. None wish to. 'The question is,' Brearley said, 'how thin your skin needs to be. You need to be sensitive enough to let everything come through – but not so sensitive you are overwhelmed.'

When I called him on his hols in Antigua this week, Gower said: 'It depends on how prepared you are to keep it simple; on how easy you find it to relegate the obvious hassles to the fourth division; on how sensitive you want to be; on how easy you find it to keep things like Pakistani umpires in perspective. Your communication skills are the most useful thing in the job, perhaps. And the hardest part of the job is the amount of time you must give it: days, weeks and months at a time.'

You need special attributes to be an England captain. You need the tactical acumen of Bobby Fischer, the verbal adroitness of Oscar Wilde, the diplomatic skills of the Pope and the patience of Job. You must be able to tuck into huge slices of humble pie with a smile on your face. And, as a little extra, you need to be a first class sportsman at the peak of your game.[4]

An England captain must know how to play his heart out and then how to take all the blame. He must fulfil all the demands the job makes and then act like a jolly good sport when he gets fired. He must lead a totally outclassed side against, say, the West Indies, and get sacked when England lose. He must lead his side through the trip-wires of Caribbean politics and the culture clashes of the sub-continent and, if anything goes wrong, he must accept the sack. He must absorb all these pressures and still play like a super-hero.

He must combine an impossible number of talents and know all the time that if he makes the smallest error or suffers the slightest misfortune he will be dumped on from a dizzy height. The public and the media will do their share but his employers, the TCCB, will lead the way every time.[5]

Mothers, have the highest ambitions for your sons. But if you love them, do not wish the England captaincy on them.

[1] This was a reference to Gatting's reverse sweep, which got him dismissed in the World Cup final.
[2] Gatting felt the lash of that particular truth the following summer.
[3] The word was 'grovel'.
[4] I read all this paragraph over to Gower, unsure of what his reaction would be. I was pleased when he said he agreed absolutely.
[5] Really, I can claim this as a successful prophecy, can't I?

PART 6

THE TIMES 1988

I went to cover the Mike Tyson–Larry Holmes fight rather against my will, and with a technicolour burst of flu to cheer things along. The result was that I did not feel in the mood for mincing my words. In fact, my reporting became a sustained tirade of vituperation. The next Sunday, Alan Hubbard wrote the following paragraph in *The Observer*: 'Larry Holmes was not alone in feeling sick as a pugilist after last weekend's world title fight. At the ringside *The Times* representative, a somewhat sensitive soul, was left ashen-faced and seemed about to throw up after witnessing the savagery inflicted by Mike Tyson. "I never want to cover another boxing match," he vowed to askance-looking colleagues. Doubtless this will interest the paper's regular boxing correspondent, whom they had decided not to send.' With an endorsement like that, how could I do anything but include all three pieces I wrote about the fight?

A GAME THAT IS MORE OF A MYTH THAN A HIT
January 1988

Atlantic City: Boxing is the great preserve of the myth-makers. No other sport has quite the same urge to create its own legends. Myths are its business: myths are, above all, box-office. That is why boxing is quite delighted with Mike Tyson. And as Tyson, aged 21, moves towards his classic confrontation with the former champion, Larry Holmes, aged 38, all those with a vested interest in the sport will be quietly praying for Tyson.

There is already a legend building up around Tyson: a legend of atavistic violence, of unstoppable, rhinoceros-charging destruction. He began his professional career with 19 successive knockouts, all but five of them in the first round. He became World Boxing Council world heavyweight champion in 1986 and last year became the undisputed champion, combining the entire alphabet soup of titles when he beat Tony Tucker.

Tyson is an awesome boxer, no doubt about that. But many people want him to be better than that: they want him to be one of the all-time greats. Boxing needs – well, not another Ali, there could never be two of him and, anyway, Ali kept making his own rules up in everything he approached. Boxing needs another legend; better still, one easier to deal with than Ali. And Tyson is doing his best to be the man.

His explosive three years have caught the public's imagination, enlivened public interest in boxing and packed in the high rollers at ghastly places like Las Vegas and Atlantic City. When Tyson fights, the thousand-buck-a-hand merchants come to town. Tyson is someone people want to watch, read about, write about.

His startling aggression is part of it but this is made more intriguing by his contradictory Press conference persona: the quiet voice, the lisp, the rather sweet little jokes. When he gets into the ring he seems to put a completely different head on: a frightening, snarling, apparently quite personal aggression. He doesn't look like a man there to take part in a sporting event at all: he looks like a man seeking violence for the simple pleasure of it.

Then the charm again, the gap-toothed smile with a little twinkle of gold. Tyson seems a made-to-measure boxing legend: the wild boy from the ghetto tamed for our enjoyment. And all it took was several million dollars. The legend of Tyson's rackety past gets a little better with every fight. A childhood of unabashed criminality. 'As a kid I carried a gun,' he has been quoted as saying. 'All the gangs had guns back in Brownsville, Brooklyn. They used them in hold-ups and in gang fights. The fights only started with fists. Then the guns and knives came out. Sure, I fired mine. Thank God I never hit anybody.'

Tyson is, in short, the personification of one of boxing's greatest pieces of self-justification: that boxing is 'a way out of the ghetto.' Let us put to one side the ludicrous aspect of this claim: the implicit notion that there is a job as heavyweight champion of the world waiting for all kids from tough backgrounds, if only they could get their acts together.

For there is something more than merely silly in the notion. The success of one brilliantly talented athlete seems somehow to excuse the fact that ghettos exist at all. One magical story about a legendary boxer makes the whole question of poverty seem to evaporate. After all, how can there be anything wrong with a place that produces such a man?

With such men as Tyson violence is sanctified and the ghetto background glamourised. No wonder so many powerful people love him: no wonder, by the same token, that so many powerful people hated Ali. Ali refused to play the game: he gave up his 'slave name' of Clay, he refused to be drafted. They jailed him, stripped him of his world championship and banned him from trying to win it back. You can see how important the legend of the good boxer is by the way they treat the boxers who won't go along with it: Jack Johnson was vilified just as Ali was. Tyson is moving towards the status of an acceptable legend and tomorrow's fight, youthful fury against the ageing giant, has every aspect of drama you could wish for.

Ah, there is no sport like boxing, people tell me, no sport that produces such characters, such confrontations, such awesome contests. There is a simple reason for this. Most man-to-man sports are a form of stylised duelling – with a racket and a ball, or whatever. The enmity, the attacking, the defending are all metaphorical.

There is no metaphor in boxing: it is the real thing. Boxing is real fighting, perfectly genuine violence, a pastime whose perfectly genuine aim is to cause brain damage in the opponent. No wonder the contests stir the blood: no wonder the contestants are awesome, mythic men. The point is not, in fact, that 'there is no sport like boxing.' The point is that boxing is not a sport at all. It is violence unadulterated, performed for the pleasure of millions. And millions is what it is all about.

HOLMES FEELS LIKE ANOTHER $1M
January 1988

If Las Vegas has pretentions to a tawdry sense of style, Atlantic City has pretentions to being a tawdry kind of Las Vegas. To take a stroll on the boardwalk, the wooden-floored seafront promenade, is to suffer a curious feeling of intrusion. I seem to be the youngest person here by about 30 years and the lightest by about 130 lb.

I suppose that does, at least, make this horrid place a suitable venue for Larry Holmes' eccentric attempt to win back the world heavyweight championship tonight. Holmes is a grandfather and weighs in at a ridiculously over-the-top 38 years. He is challenging the sensational Mike Tyson, who is 21 and already a legend of ferocity.

But why? That is the puzzler. The answer, $3.1 million (about £1.75 million), really will not do. Holmes is not doing too badly when it comes to dollars. Larry Holmes Inc owns $10 million-worth of hotel and the company is building a $10 million apartment and office complex, in, yes, Larry Holmes Drive, Easton, Pennsylvania. There is plenty more to the empire. Holmes has a home worth $1.5 million and owns cars, lorries and motorbikes worth a further million. He is not, it seems, trading a beating for a new fortune.

In one sense he is perfectly capable of continuing as he is. But it seems he cannot bear to do it. And so he is taking the appalling risk in this appallingly dangerous game of getting his brains knocked out by the awesome young champion for some twisted sense of pride and resentment.

Holmes has not boxed since April 1986 when he was beaten controversially by Michael Spinks. His only other defeat was the equally controversial beating by the same man in September 1985. These were his last two contests and they spoilt his record, which is now 48-2. Holmes believes that the world now sees him as a kind of non-champion. Sure, he was heavyweight champion of the world but one of the forgotten ones. The only truly memorable thing he did was to defeat Muhammad Ali: a fight remembered not because Holmes won but because Ali lost. It was the end of an era. Ali was 38.

But it was not the start of a new era. It was an interregnum. Holmes was just doing his bit as the championship was kept warm for the ferocious child with the 19¾in neck: Mike Tyson, the new, beloved legend. And that conventionally accepted view of recent boxing history is the worm in the Holmes gut.

Tyson has fought 32 times and many of his opponents – all beaten, mind you – have been pretty ordinary boxers. And yet Tyson is hailed as a new godling. 'He ain't no superman,' Holmes said. 'If he fought all those guys that were around when I was coming up – Shavers, Norton, Williams, Ali, Frazier – they'd have kicked the crap out of him. He was made for those guys. He is a face fighter. He's made for me. My left jab will be in his face all night long.'

The view of those not wholly won over by the myth is that Tyson is a crude and limited fighter. He packs aggression and power that overwhelms but he does not outthink or outbox his opponents. Some thoughtful observers agree that Holmes would probably have beaten Tyson in his younger days. But these are not Holmes' younger days; these are his older days. 'To beat Tyson, it would take a good left, with lateral movement – two of the things I do best,' he said. Or did best.

In some ways Holmes is in good shape: burning with resentment, a chip the size of the Trump Plaza Hotel on his shoulder and an arrogant belief in his superiority. He has always had a reputation of being a smart fighter. He is likely to come out with an intelligent and workable game-plan. The doubt is whether he will be able to carry it out.

It is quite easy to outthink a steamroller but it gets hard when the thing is on top of you. Tyson's aggression blinds attempts to outthink him. But the main question is physical: whether Holmes' body will carry him through the ferocious pounding he will certainly endure.

He is yearning for immortality, for what he sees as justice. He wants to be seen as a really special boxer, not the man who happened between Ali and Tyson. To win the championship back: only Floyd Patterson, Tim Witherspoon and Ali have done that. That would show them.

He has been passed fit for the bout. There was a lot of talk about the excellence of his condition at the Press conference. In the past a doctor had told him that he risked paralysis by fighting: a possible herniated disc was then putting pressure on a neck nerve.

There is always the possibility of an upset, a chance that Holmes will get his own back on the world. But there is also the possibility that this will be a horror show, a night that shames boxing, a night that makes decent people want to throw up. The potential is there for the kind of hideousness that a mismatch can provide. If that is what happens, Holmes can comfort himself with the thought that a lot of people have made a great deal of money from his hammering; including himself, of course. I do not know how much comfort the thought will bring him.

COUNTING THE COST OF A FATAL ATTRACTION
January 1988

Atlantic City: It looked horrible on television but, believe me, at ringside it was infinitely worse. Mike Tyson's fourth-round assault on Larry Holmes was certainly the most savage thing I have ever seen in the name of sport. And boxing experts either side of me were saying the same thing. The difference was that they were speaking with approval: with enthusiasm. Me, I was wondering whether or not to throw up.

The facts: Tyson retained the undisputed world heavyweight championship on Friday night by knocking out Holmes after two minutes and 55 seconds of the fourth

175

round. Holmes, the former champion, was the man who ended Muhammad Ali's career when Ali tried yet another last hurrah at the age of 38. Holmes is now 38, and this is no age to fight people like Tyson.

Holmes was destroyed for the entertainment of millions across the world. No, this was not sport, this was an entertainment: for the referee, Joe Cortez, let the fight continue well after the result was in no doubt. The audience must get its money's worth: that is what this game is all about.

Holmes was not pathetic, far from it. Two of the three judges gave him the third round. In the fourth round he was dancing, jabbing – and then got caught. He went down, got at once to his feet (on a count of four) and was given a count to eight standing, shaking his head to clear it, apparently already concussed.

Tyson came in again, inevitably caught him again. Holmes, with unbelievable courage, was up again on five, counted again to eight. Tyson burrowed in on his man once again, landing a frightening succession of punches. Holmes was finished, clearly beaten, obviously concussed, but was still standing. Just.

Cortez watched as Tyson finished the job: a succession of gratuitous blows that were needed not for victory but for the satisfaction and delight of the fighting world. When Holmes finally reached the canvas and did not rise, for a moment I thought he might even have been killed.

The power of the heavyweight is not truly apparent on television. It is only at ringside that the immensity, the power of these men comes over. Tyson is one of the most powerful men on earth: according to the dictates of the sport of boxing, it was right and proper for him to aim a succession of blows at the brain of a defenceless man.

Afterwards, the helpers seemed to have trouble removing Holmes' mouthpiece, and there was a suggestion from some observers that Holmes was swallowing his tongue. But Holmes was up in the end, after a worrying wait, and was able to leave the ring on his own legs, however shaky they were. For Holmes it was something he will never forget. Note: a Harley Street neurologist told me that concussion *always* brings with it permanent brain damage. Thus to assault the brain of your opponent and to do it permanent damage is the ultimate aim of any participant in the sport of boxing.

Tyson is unquestionably a superb athlete and a deeply awesome man. He is only 21 and the champion, the winner of 33 professional fights, the loser of none. 'Screw the money, screw everything. I just want to fight. Fight to the finish,' he said. The legend of Tyson grows, and the juggernaut of boxing rolls on ever faster. If, occasionally, too-fervent worshippers such as Holmes are crushed between its wheels, the progress of the juggernaut is uninterrupted. There is always another man with dreams of the future, or dreams of the past, to step forward.

Poor Holmes: but it is ever thus for those who suffer from the dreaded Freddie Trueman disease: the sincere belief that the products of the modern age are all incompetent second-raters when compared with the people of the golden age of their youth. Perhaps more than anything, they cannot bear to relinquish the spotlight of attention: the applause, being at the centre of a gathering of high rollers and fancy ladies.

Sportsmen are always trying to make comebacks: it is part of the rhythm of every sporting year. Perhaps they cannot stand the drabness of living forever in the shadow of their own youth. Always they believe it is possible to find within themselves one more last hurrah.

To meet a man like Tyson at such a moment is a dreadful thing. When Holmes fought Ali eight years ago, he showed mercy. He refused to destroy the man in his power. Tyson had no such squeamishness. Holmes may have earned $3.1 million, but he earned it desperately hard.

From the Diary

An American gentleman got so excited watching the Olympic ice hockey – yes, really – that he shot himself. Paul Grant, aged 18, of Paducah, Kentucky, was putting his pistol away while watching the United States play Czechoslovakia. But as he did so, the American team scored a goal. Grant said: 'I tensed up, and the gun went off.' He shot himself in the hand with a .38 bullet, but the doctors say he is not permanently hurt.

> *The Times* sports editor, Tom Clarke, most uncharacteristically, was consumed by a deep and humourless loathing for Eddie Edwards. Faced with such a clear indication of official policy, what could I do but write the following piece?

MAN ON THE SIDE OF THE ANGELS
February 1988

Even as I write, waves of vitriolic hate are flowing towards Eddie Edwards. People have started to speak the name of the British ski jumping record holder through clenched teeth. And the East Germans are apoplectic about him, calling him in one of their laughter-packed newspapers 'a self-publicising clown.'

There is the nationalistic argument for hating Edwards: that his participation makes Britain look like a bastion of nurds and incompetent buffoons in beer-bottle specs: England, the spiritual home of sloppy amateurism. But I never did think much of nationalistic argument.

There is the sanctity of sport argument: that Edwards' very participation somehow profanes the sacred flame. If anyone believes that sport (let alone a kind of *Jeux sans Frontières* on man-made snow and ice) is a religion, I suggest a spiritual reappraisal.

Then there is the argument that Edwards is unfair to his fellow competitors: that he is stealing the limelight from all the worthy biathletes and lugers and downhillers. I expect many of the British team do feel rather miffed: but that is their problem. Do they really imagine that but for Edwards the British Nordic ski team would be making world headlines?

And actually the other ski jumpers have been saying some nice things about Edwards. He has made their event the Olympic No 1 and because of all the fuss about Edwards an enormous number of people have seen the amazing jumping of Matti Nykaenen. Because of the contrast – Edwards has made the event a kind of pro-am – you can for once see how awesomely difficult the event really is.

Edwards has provoked delighted affection and wild, irrational hatred: people are spitting with rage about his very presence at the Games. I find this odd. For, in fact, Britain has plenty of other no-hopers in Calgary. The thing is that Edwards is the *story*. He just happened to be a journalist's dream in an Olympics that was, for most of its audience, long on incomprehensibles and short on personalities.

The whole Edwards story has got wildly out of hand, of course. But don't blame Eddie. He is not a deliberate self-publiciser: no one could have created that kind of global interest cynically. Certainly, he rather loves the attention now he has got it: what sportsman would not? But he is just riding the media wave.

It so happened that in a dull Games, Edwards was a walking story: with his Gloucestershire burr, his gameness, his eccentricity, and, above all, his glasses. He could never have achieved fame without the glasses: he looks wonderfully incongruous in his photographs, and the finishing touch, the fact that they mist up when he sets off and 'I just have to hope they clear by the time I reach the bottom,' has given delight to the whole world.

Now the story has gone into overdrive, and from there into reverse, and people are queuing up to condemn Edwards. But the problem is not Edwards: it is with the Edwards story. You can't blame Edwards for revelling in it, nor begrudge the fact that he might make a few quid from all the nonsense. Good luck to him, even if he does seem rather to play up to his own new-minted cliché.

But don't condemn him for taking part in the Olympics and

doing his poor best in them. Or are the modern Olympics no
for the taking part but for the winning?

Here is my Katarina Witt piece. It is only right to add
that my wife completely disagrees with me in what I say
about skating ... but not in what I say about Katarina.

KATARINA SKATES IN AS CHAMPION
EVERY TIME
February 1988

So there I was, sitting in a bar in France last Monday, reading
a magazine on the cover of which was a picture of a gir
wearing the most unbelievable black leather knickers, a butch
black leather jacket, and a quite ravishing smile.

But what, I hear you ask, is so unusual about that? Nothing
really – except that this was an article about sport. It wa:
headlined *L'art Erotique de Katarina Witt*: Katarina is the mos
fancied contender for the gold medal in the women's figure
skating, and she will do her *Carmen* routine tonight
tempestuous, graceful and *très, très érotique*. The magazine wa:
a delightful read: '*Elle flirte avec les juges*,' it said. It recounted
a tale of the time her costume was so skimpy that one of her
breasts popped free in mid-skate: the magazine commented
lubriciously: '*difficile d'être plus glasnost*.'

Katarina is great, splendid and wonderful, there is nc
disputing that: a stunning performer, an electric showbi:
personality. But what on earth is she doing at the Olympics:
Why is a kind of ballet pretending to be a sport? Skating's bes
gift to sport has been a joke. When I dive and miss a catch
behind the stumps, one of the slips is quite certain to say.
'Nought for the catch, but a perfect six for artistic
impression.'

180

Artistic impression! How ludicrous! Leonardo's 'Helicopter' in the original set pattern scored 1.8 for technical merit but a big 5.9 for artistic impression. In the free programme, can we expect a perfect six for his Madonna of the Rocks?

The thing about skating is that all of it is bad sport and practically all of it is bad art. If a sport needs arbitrary marks for 'artistic impression' it is not a real sport at all. And if it needs the tang of competition to make it work, then it is seriously lacking as an art.

That is my theory, anyway, and like all theories, it works perfectly until exceptional people come along to spoil it. Torvill and Dean were just such people: cuckoos in the nest of suburbia. When people with such gifts pour all they have into four minutes of time, they tend to produce something worth looking at. With Torvill and Dean, spectators and judges alike gave up thinking about competition: it was flowers and sixes all the way.

The memorable performers in ice skating of every discipline are those that break the mould of competition, who skate not for marks but for the beauty of it. No one will remember boring old Bestemianova and Bukin's Passion-by-Numbers-Part-33: the class act was the Duchesnays, never mind their rotten marks, they made an artistic impression on the audience all right.

But if the sport is nonsense, Katarina is an unadulterated treat. I remember speaking to an up-and-coming skater a few years ago, and she said: 'People say: "She's got a triple this, or a triple that, so she'll win". It shouldn't be like that. You should be able just to look at her skate past, and say, wow, she's a champion.'

It has happened: that is Katarina through and through. Never mind the marks, never mind the flirtatiousness and the flagrant sexiness: every movement she makes on the ice is wonderful to watch. The flaw with the average skater is the arms: used as rigid balancing poles, with the occasional harried gesture as a concession to 'artistry'. But Katarina flows. If she skated with a paper bag on her head, she would still be a star. The sport is silly, but I wouldn't miss her tonight for the world.

The Hong Kong Sevens has since 1976 been the best rugby tournament in the world. Well, Andy Ripley agrees with me for a start. I used to live in Hong Kong, stayed there four years, and both the place and the competition have a kind of magic about them. This piece is a fairly straightforward celebration of both.

WHY THE LABEL DOES NOT COUNT
March 1988

Hong Kong: 'Made in Hong Kong' still carries a certain sting to it. So perhaps it is best not to point out that the Rugby World Cup, an event that had sports people all over the world crowing with delight, was actually made in Hong Kong. For the first real gathering of the rugby nations *en masse* happened in Hong Kong in 1976.

This was the first Hong Kong Sevens: it was initially sponsored by Rothmans, but someone there decided it was a bad idea. Perhaps it was the same man who turned down the Beatles at Decca: the event has grown quite prodigiously, and now carries the power title of the Cathay Pacific Hong Kong Bank Invitation Sevens. What is more, it has become that rare thing, an event loved by players, spectators and sponsors all together. It is, in short, a Great Hong Kong Success Story.

And the Sevens remains an event to revel in: I covered it several times for local publications when I lived here, and coming back now for the third time to cover it for this paper, I find myself in tremendous spirits. For there are major matters to consider: will Fiji do it again? They play sevens the way Brazilians play football, and it's wonderful to behold. But I remember when they got turned over by South Korea in a ridiculous underdog game: that was pretty wondrous, too, and maybe Sri Lanka will win the plate competition again: it is not every day that Sri Lanka win an international rugby trophy.

Until I first went to the Hong Kong Sevens, I had no idea that rugby was played outside the five nations and the old colonies. But despite itself, rugby has become a truly international game. This year there are teams from the United States, Papua New Guinea, Spain, Italy, Tonga, Taiwan, Singapore, Malaysia, Thailand and plenty of other places where you would not believe they had heard of the game. Nor is the Hong Kong Sevens glorious only for its obscurity: there will be an Australian and a New Zealand side: national sides I mean, with green and gold or black shirts, and appropriately stern countenances.

Of course, the home unions won't play ball, and though I dislike the reasons they have for keeping the national sides away – pure snootiness – I can't help but think it is a good thing. There are more English people in the crowd than any other brand: the lack of a true home team makes the event not nationalistic but truly and splendidly international.

True, the Hong Kongers could shout for Hong Kong but mostly they don't. In fact, many of them will actually be shouting for Papua New Guinea when they meet Hong Kong tomorrow: to see the underdogs beat the ex-pats will give everyone a moment of pleasure. But most of the Hong Kongers will be rooting for Fiji: flare, dynamism, individualism, explosiveness: all the things, in fact, that I most like about Hong Kong itself. A crowd of white men yelling their heads off for Fiji is one of those things that gives a sportswriter a rare moment of optimism.

In fact, the entire event tends to do that. The players seem to have a perfect attitude to it: perhaps because this is sevens and not the cumbersome 15-man version of the game. They know that results can be freaky, and anyone can get turned over by just about anyone. Above all, they know it is 'just' sevens and not the Real Thing. They go out there to try their damnedest, but mostly they don't go out as if to war. The event retains a certain air of carnival about it: it is the sort of carnival that everyone wants to win, of course, but it actually is true that even more than winning, the players want to be there, to take part. And it is not often one can write that.

You might think it is impossible to have an international

event without nationalism or needle. In fact, I can't think of another event that manages it: but this is an unusual competition, and Hong Kong is an unusual place. I think both are great: but then I have always thought 'Made in Hong Kong' is a label to wear with pride.

There is more to being a winner than being able to do it better than everyone else. To be a winner, a major, consistent and inevitable winner, year after year, requires extraordinary mental strength, and a very special relationship with the sport and with life. Accordingly, I put together a series of interviews with three such legends of their sport: Steve Davis, Bill Shoemaker and Nelson Piquet: snooker player, jockey and racing car driver. All three turned out, in their vastly different ways, to be fascinating interview subjects. And yes, I did find something in common between them, and it was not at all what I expected.

WHY DAVIS IS HOOKED ON WINNING
April 1988

Most people believe the lot of a top athlete is enviable. You get love and adulation everywhere you go and get paid a fortune, all for doing something you love. Surely that beats the hell out of working for a living.

It is also widely accepted that sportspeople are often boorish, cantankerous, moody, aggressive, sulky and generally prone to acting the spoilt brat. Naturally, people get furious with them; how can athletes behave so badly when their lot is so utterly enviable?

The answer to this conundrum is simple: being an athlete is not, in truth, easy. Athletes are probably the twitchiest, most insecure people in the world: their ultra-defensiveness, their boorishness, their regular fits of utter gracelessness all come down to the same thing: a highly competitive job makes people horribly jumpy and insecure. And there is no more competitive job than competition.

It is not the money, or not just the money. Athletes do not think about money at all, not when they play. Mostly, they play with a frightening obsession with winning, or, as often, with a frightening obsession with defeat, and how they might avoid it.

'I haven't got any interests,' Steve Davis said.

'You find snooker that absorbing?' I asked.

'I do. I'm a freak, in that way, I suppose. Because obviously nobody else finds it as absorbing as I do.'

'Well – what do you enjoy most in the world?'

'I'm probably at my happiest when I've been playing badly. And then I get down on the practice table and it all starts to come back – like a revelation. And that is something that's forever going on, you're forever going out of tune. And every time you do it, it's ah! Bloody 'ell, I've been standing a bit wrong. And it all falls into place, and I think, cor! I'm looking forward to the next tournament.'

Everyone who has ever watched a British woman play at Wimbledon knows that the ability to win is quite different to the ability to play well. Davis said: 'People say, "I'd rather play well and lose than play badly and win." That's all very well, but you're more pleased with yourself if you've played badly and won. To me, that's a much more important thing to do. *Winning* is the constant confirmation that you are doing your job right. And if you don't get this reassurance, you start to doubt. If you talk to winners, you get a very positive attitude – you should talk to winners who have since become losers.'

'Well,' I said, 'you've been there yourself, haven't you?' I was referring to what is probably the most famous snooker match ever played, in which Davis was defeated on the last black by Dennis Taylor for the world championship in 1985.

'Yes. The trauma of that defeat was a lot bigger than anything else. I remember the couple of days after. I remember when it hit me, in the bath, I had a big depression in the bath. But the thing is, I've always been basically optimistic. I've never looked back at things that were bad. I've always tried to work out *why* they were bad – and then do something about it.'

In that awesome game against Taylor, Davis had his chance at the black. He missed, of course. 'Funnily enough, I don't regret missing the ball. I think you are allowed to miss balls. It is much more of a problem if you start to *think* wrong. I am much more worried if I miscount the score, than if I miss a ball. You're allowed to play bad shots. But if you play a bad *tactical* shot, through panic, then it's a real kick in the nuts, a real blow to your confidence.

'It is rare to see a player go totally out the window. When you do, it is not because they are missing balls, but because they are not thinking right. They go for a pot when they should be playing safety, because they are desperate to get a ball in; they play a safety shot when they should have attacked, because they are frightened of missing ... once you lose the happiness in your game, you start to think wrong.'

Davis came back from the Taylor game to re-establish himself as the dominant force in the game. In the previous season he scarcely lost a match: he bestrides the modern game like a colossus. Every tournament is a further test of his dominance: but it is his relish for that constant testing of his ability and his will that is crucial to his success. Indeed, it is more than crucial: it is intoxicating to him, and, in the final analysis, quite addictive.

He goes into every tournament, every match, with the same renowned death's head seriousness: 'I have to. A lot of people don't like my attitude, but it is the only way I can guarantee that my mind is totally on the job. I have to take things away from myself, like a monk.'

'There is a clear difference between you and the other players, always.'

'That's the way I like it to be. I feel that if I were to enjoy myself at a tournament, I'd get worried. If I started enjoying things outside snooker, at a tournament, then I'd worry that I was not enjoying the snooker. Like if you go to a film before you go to the dentist: it's because you don't really want to go to the dentist at all. I feel that a lot of the players would really rather not be at the tournament.'

'But you like the whole process?'

'The thrill I get from the game is the preparation, like the revision for an exam – and the *doing* of it. I enjoy preparing myself, I enjoy the continual test. People say, "You've won the world championship, you've earned a lot of money, you can't need anything else." But it doesn't work like that. You want to test yourself again. It's like a drug. The adrenalin you produce becomes an addiction.'

'So the process of winning a tournament involves turning yourself into a monomaniac for the duration of the event?'

'Exactly. And I get depressed after every tournament. Whether I win or lose. It's always an anti-climax. I am more depressed if I lose, sure, but I get a depression of a certain type when I win. Because it's finished, you see.'

'You are easily the best player when it comes to winning tournaments. Are there players with greater abilities at simply playing snooker?'

'Yes. Many. In different ways: Jimmy White's cue power, Cliff Thorburn's concentration, Willie Thorne's break-building, Joe Johnson's fluency, Neal Foulds' long potting, Dennis Taylor's tactical ability.'

The list is produced with alarming fluency. 'But the thing with me is that I have a good average at everything, like Gary Sobers. I mentioned all those players with greater abilities than mine in certain areas: I still would not decry my own abilities in those areas. A graph of my abilities would be a straight line: about 75 per cent at everything. I have no weaknesses. Other players will have graphs like this.' And Davis sketched a profile in the air of the Andes. 'And this is something I have always aimed at, always worked on.'

'So we are back with technique, and practice?'

'Yes. And the luck of the temperament.'

'Which is also something you have worked at.'

'I think I have used it to my advantage – but I was also born with it!'

It is the mechanics of the game that absorbs Davis. All golfers are obsessed by their game's mechanics: Davis is constantly amazed that the same overriding concern does not exist in snooker. Davis' taste for self-analysis, of his game and of his own nature, has created the method for his success.

A normal player will practise every bit as much as Davis, but he will tend to spend more time smacking balls about, enjoying making centuries, or what have you: rather like a concert pianist practising by playing his favourite tunes. Davis is a meticulous player of scales and arpeggios and five-finger exercises: 'It's beneficial, it's therapeutic, and I love doing it. Because my enjoyment is not necessarily in the winning, but in the *doing* of it.'

UNBRIDLED JOY OF EASY RIDER
April 1988

If you concentrate on the athletes at the very top of the top you give yourself an easy time. Because at this dizzy, stratospheric level of achievement you simply do not find any 'side'. Side is the preserve of the second-raters, the people who have clawed every step of their way, who have had to make the very most out of every single ounce of ability they possess: admirable people in many ways, full of blood and guts and determination, but people who have just a tiny corner of disappointment with themselves.

This tends to come out, not in inner sadness, but in side. It is only the truly great that need no swagger, who need never insist on their own superiority. Certainly this is true of Bill Shoemaker, the most successful jockey of all time, and arguably the most successful sportsman of all time.

He is 56, stands at four foot eleven and has ridden nearly 9,000 winners. No other jockey is even close to that total. As a comparison, Piggott rode 5,191 winners. And Shoemaker is still riding. He is the most affable man you could wish to meet and, despite his unusual size, he has more self-possession than any of the shifty-eyed giants among the second-raters in every sport. He specialises in the highly American habit of drawling understatement: ain't no big deal, winning all them races. Eclipse awards? Someone's got to get 'em, I guess.

Charles Whittingham, 'The Bald Eagle,' is another American racing legend and, as a trainer, he has had his best successes in partnership with Shoemaker. Unsurprisingly, he is something of an authority on the man: 'You have to realise that he is a perfect athlete. Great at tennis, great golf player: he has perfect co-ordination. If he'd been a little bigger he could easily have been a champion golfer. He does *everything* well.'

But the truly remarkable thing about Shoemaker's riding is not, apparently, athleticism but the fact that he seems to do nothing at all on his horse. Not much that you can see, anyway: monkey-wriggle acrobatics and machine-gun whippings are not his style. He just gets on a horse and it goes. If you take a walk around Santa Anita racetrack of a morning to watch the work, people will queue up to tell you tales of Shoemaker's uncanny horsemanship: a rogue animal will scatter his work riders like confetti, but put Shoemaker on top and they are instantly transformed into lambs.

'Oh, yeah, I play with him, fool around, you know? He responds, he knows I'm trying to be nice – I guess, anyway. Play with the bit, give and take. Touch, I guess – that's my theory.'

Shoemaker is utterly without the traditional bitterness of the jockey. It is a pleasure to have a beer with him – and you can. Unlike most jockeys, he can have a beer any time he wants. He has no weight problems and that tends to make for a saner outlook than that of the grim victims of wasting. And he is wholly without the standard jockey's chip about physique: his build has been a priceless asset to him.

Naturally, it was his size that made people suggest he become a jockey. 'So how did it start?' I asked him. 'Weren't any big deal. I was going to high school, girl in my class was dating a jockey, she said, why don't you become a jockey? I said, what the hell's a jockey? I was 15 or so, got a job on a ranch, taking care of horses, cleaning out stalls ...'

'And was there a moment when you realised that you had something special? That you had something that other riders lacked?'

'No, I never thought about it in that way. But I knew as

soon as I got to the ranch, working with those horses, I knew that was what I enjoyed. That was what I was going to do. And I took to it like a duck to water. I worked there for a year before I got on a horse. First time I got on one, that was a great thrill.

'I started riding races in 1949. Right away I had a great rapport with the animals. They liked me. We got on well together. I got along with them better than the big guys, who fought them all the time. I would kind of give and take with them and they galloped for me better than for the other guys.'

But how did he make that happen? 'I don't know. A rapport, a kind of sixth sense, I don't know. The animal and I, we have a feeling for each other. That's sort of it.'

'Have you ever been frightened on a horse?'

'Oh, yeah. You bet. The thing about fear is, you've got to be able to talk yourself out of it. Everyone gets scared. I say to myself, if you're scared, don't do it. Quit. But I want to do it! So, don't be scared. Worst thing that happened, horse fell on me, broke my pelvis in five places, bladder, all kinds of internal things. You name it, it's happened. But I'm still here, yeah?'

Shoemaker is so perfectly relaxed a person that it is hard to believe he is a professional sportsman. He has none of the sportsman's occupational disease of insecurity. Partly, this is because of his unbelievable achievements, partly it is his age, but mostly, it is because this is his nature, anyway.

'Oh, but he's competitive all right,' Whittingham said. 'You play golf with him, you find that out. But he can switch it on and off when he wants.'

'So many sportsmen are pretty obsessive,' I said to Shoemaker. 'But you don't seem that way at all.'

'That's true. I'm an easygoing kind of a guy and I do my job and I like to play with the other guys in the jockey's room. I think that's part of it. If you can't have fun doing what you're doing, well, get out. And you can have fun and do a good job – at least, I can. Some guys can't. Sometimes I make some joke to another guy in the race. He says "Shut up, you're disturbing my concentration." These guys have a different outlook.'

190

Shoemaker is an unflagging josher, an insuppressible kidder. He likes to laugh and joke and tease before, after and during a race. Relaxation is that easy for him. There was a famous occasion back in his youth when he forgot where the winning post was, and in a major race; he stopped riding for a few strides, thinking he had won, realised he had stopped too soon, kicked on again – and was caught on the line.

In the next big race of that season his reputation was on the line, his big race temperament in question. The night before, he had dined with a fellow jockey, and the two of them had boasted about their chances in the race. This jockey hit the front and Shoemaker set off after him. He drew alongside and then he just could not resist the jape. He deliberately checked his horse, and said 'Hey! How y'doin'?' Then, roaring with laughter, he kicked on for victory.

That, I think, is pretty high-calibre relaxation. 'You should be that way. Too tense, you probably do something you shouldn't. I've got more relaxed over the years but I started off pretty relaxed, too – probably more so than the other guys. I have fun. More so than anything. I knew I could ride, I never did worry about making a mistake or losing.'

'Do you get excited when you win?'

'Not necessarily so, no. I've kind of trained myself over the years not to get too high and not to get too low. That's the game: one time you're way up here, next time way down there. Sometimes you get beat in a big race, it affects your riding the next horse. I try not to let that happen. I think I've trained myself to do that thing over the years.'

'So how many more years are you going to keep it up?'

'Well, I've been threatening to quit for about 10 years but I've never got around to it. I enjoy doing it, I enjoy the camaraderie, it keeps me young, you know? I enjoy racing. I might be off for a couple of days and it's always nice to get back out there ... riding a nice coupla horses ...'

PIQUET FUELLED BY PURE GENIUS
April 1988

Every Brit knows who Nelson Piquet is: he is the beastly, much too good-looking foreigner (a Brazilian, actually) who stops our nice Nigel from winning the world motor racing championship. But real motor racing men have a different attitude to him.

The other week I wrote about a skater who said she didn't care too much about jumps and pyrotechnics: 'I want to be someone who just skates past and people say, "Wow, she must be the champion." ' Piquet is a bit like that for motor racing people: a pure, pared-down, effortless, graceful talent. Those who appreciate the genuine subtleties of the driver's art would sooner see a single lap of Piquet's micrometer-precision driving than any amount of gung ho, barnstorming heroics from, well, Nigel Mansell, Britain's ever-heroic second best.

Mansell is a great talent, no question about that, and he might even win the championship this year, who knows. But the difference is that he has had to work and work to get there, to become as good as he is. For Piquet, the whole lot was God-given. Mansell is a talent in the Kevin Keegan class: Piquet is from the George Best school of pure, natural ability.

And Piquet is a winner, a natural winner. He has won the world championship three times. That puts him alongside Stewart, Brabham and Lauda. Only Fangio has won it more times. Piquet is in pretty rarefied company.

Piquet is not just handsome and talented and rich. He also has a clear nutty streak. He has shiny brown eyes that dart about the place, looking for something to interest him. He recently joined Team Lotus, which is sponsored by Camel cigarettes. Piquet is a non-smoker but when his new car was unveiled he carried a cigarette into the Press conference and pretended to smoke it. A mild joke. But Piquet took a quiet, disproportionate pleasure in it, bringing it to his lips and knocking imaginary ash into a real ashtray for quite half an hour. I found this bizarre.

Piquet is an original. He is one of those sportsmen who

seems to reinvent the game as he goes. 'I enjoy everything made in the top,' he said, in his vivid, idiosyncratic English. 'Every sport made good, I appreciate. The other day I was looking at the ballet skating on television – this, personally, I do not like, but the thing is so well done, they are so well prepared, that I love to see it.'

'The point about sport is excellence?'

'Yes.'

Excellence was what I had gone to the Paul Ricard circuit in the south of France to talk about. Like: how come Piquet is so exceptional?

'I don't think I am exceptional.'

'Come on.'

'I am consistent. It is very easy, to do a good year and be a world champion – well, not very easy, but not so difficult. If you are in Formula One you have the talent already. So if you have the right car, and the right team, you can win. To win three times means I am very consistent for many, many years. I have been in Formula One for nine years and for five of those years I was in the top three. Other years, I was doing everything right but the car was not ready, or there were bad tyres, but if I have the chance ...

'Well, in other words, I say, I don't care what I have done, I care about what I am going to do about next season. Because I do not live with what I did when I won those championships. This season I live with what I am doing this season.' That, I think, more than anything else, spells out the difference between the professional sportsman and the sports-watcher or, for that matter, the sportswriter. We might want to meet Botham so that we can ask him about his magical 149 at Headingley: Botham will want to talk about facing the West Indies this summer. Indeed, a journalist once went to interview him and found a cricket bat lying in the rain in the garden, where his son had been playing with it. It was, yes, the bat with which he had scored that 149. Practising sportsmen are not into nostalgia: they are too eager for the next confrontation.

Patriotic Brits like to assume that Piquet is not as good as Mansell because he won only three Grands Prix last season while Lovely Nigel won six. But that is the way the points work. You might think that second place is disproportionately well rewarded but Piquet was there seven times last season. Piquet knows how the system works and drives to win not the battle but the war: not the race but the championship. He drives not for glory but for ultimate victory. He is, in a word, smart.

I asked him if there was a difference between the talent to drive and the talent to win. 'You have to be clever. Sometimes you say, I can finish second, I can finish third. You might say, I am not very good on this circuit but I can drive for some points. Of course, you need to be quick because if you are quick you start in the front and win races. And you have to be lucky – and you have always to be there. So when the opportunity comes, you win. Driving and mental strength are directly associated. If you are quick for one lap only, you do not win anything. You have to be quick *constantly*. And this is all mental.'

'What has given you the edge over Mansell?'

'Nigel is a very quick driver.'

'And you are a winner.'

'Well, in Formula One, 50 per cent of winning is the car. You have to treat the car very well to *finish* the race. Nigel is a little bit heavy on the car. The Williams car is very strong indeed, but he has sometimes done things in a race and has had to stop, because the engine, because this, because that … I am easier with the car. Much easier.'

'And this is your edge?'

'Yes. I don't have any mind preparation but what I do is, I look at the times from the Saturday, the day before the race, and see what chance I have. I see if I have a chance to win the race, or if I have to maybe settle for second and go for the points. Sometimes I see my car is two seconds quicker than any other car and I have only to go out there to win.'

Perhaps one of the things the outsider most envies about sportsmen is the fame: the way these top performers know without question that they have left some kind of mark on the world. But fame is not as much fun as it is cracked up to be: the point is that it is not something you can ever have on your own terms. Many a sportsman has courted fame quite deliberately, exploited it with all his might, and has then got miffed at the discovery that the coin has a reverse side. The name of Botham again floats irresistibly into the mind.

Piquet has, at least, been consistent. These days he does his stuff for the cameras and the tape-recorders with a good enough grace, conversing easily in a bewildering number of languages, but this is not, for him, what the job is about. 'In Brazil I have friends I have had for 15 years. I have also been in Europe for about 12 years and here I have made very few friends. I have always liked simple people. I don't give a damn for high society. I don't want to make friends with anybody who is important.'

Does he like being famous? 'No. I would prefer to have the same profession and the same enjoyment – and the same money – and nobody knows me. It is not possible, I know, but for me it would be much better.

'I think the most important thing if you want to keep going in motor racing is never to read anything. If you read bad things that people write, or you think maybe people are speaking bad things about you, you go and fight all the little details you should not fight – and then you have to stop Formula One. So first, I never read anything. Second, I am a friend of everybody. Anybody write bad things about me, next day I am talking to him, no problems. I don't make enemies.'

It is more accurate to say that he does not cultivate enemies. His bursts of temperament, his sudden stinging attacks on colleagues, do not make him universally loved. But you get the impression that Piquet has never even noticed this.

Many a sportsman has failed to make the crucial adjustment to fame but Piquet has mixed cultivated ignorance and the Garbo technique to maintain balance. He used to live on a boat that had no telephone – he is between boats right now, having a new one built. He has a telephone, too, but it is fixed for outgoing calls only.

The love of racing, of driving these unbelievable machines, shines out in his conversation: not ambition, not winning, not hunger, not complacency, just sheer involvement and love of

195

driving and racing motor cars. 'I try to have an easy life and enjoy this thing here. I try to enjoy what I am doing. That is why I am at the racetrack now, that is why I have spent 10 years in Formula One, that is why I have spent 10 years at the top – because I enjoy what I am doing so much. I like to drive, I like to be here, and everything comes so very easy for me.' It is those that love winning too well that know best the bitter taste of defeat. The true winners, the great winners, are those that love their sport for its own sake, and not as a medium for mere victory.

I have been talking with three quite amazing sportsmen, three of the greatest overachievers in sport, or in the history of sport: the ever-analytical Steve Davis, dashing Nelson Piquet and the laid-back, drawling Bill Shoemaker. Mega-winners: but if there is one thing they all share, it is not what I expected: an obsession with winning.

No, it is their quite unbridled enjoyment of the game itself: they revel not in the end, victory, but in the means, in the thing itself; for their game, for the abstract patterns of snooker, for the oily dangers of Formula One racing, for the magic of the horse, each of these men has one thing in common: an all-encompassing, overwhelming love.

In 1988, English cricket reached its nadir. The West Indies won the series 4-0, England selected four captains, and ended up barred from touring India because they eventually appointed Graham Gooch, he of South African Breweries XI fame, as captain. The twisted logic of all this was apparent early in the summer: John Emburey was selected as captain for the Lord's Test (and dropped from the side for the subsequent match). This is my response to Emburey's appointment.

REALITY BEHIND IMAGE OF EMBUREY

June 1988

Today Emburey and Gooch lead the England team out against the West Indies at Lord's. I cannot find it in my heart to rejoice for them. For a start, I am still trying to work out why Gatting was sacked as captain. True, his alleged sexual peccadilloes received spectacular publicity. But Gatting denied that they were true and the selectors accepted his word.

They sacked him, anyway. Why? Let us take the selectors literally and believe them when they say it was for the crime of having a few beers and unwisely seeking 'female company'. If this were a sackable offence, England would struggle to find 11 men eligible to play. It just happens that this binge was reported in the papers.

Let us try another tack and assume that the selectors were only pretending when they said they believed Gatting. Gatting was fired, then, for sexual irregularities. This is a private matter: it concerns Gatting and his wife. A player's private life, no matter how irregular or unsavoury, is not the selectors' business. Nor, again, would Gatting be the first England player to have sought such solace – assuming for the sake of argument that the allegations are true. In many such instances the selectors must have known about this privately: Gatting has not invented the rackety night.

It seems to me that Gatting has been fired for the unforgivable crime of getting found out. I do not find the selectors' moral stance convincing. Gatting's crime was not the rackety night but being involved in an unpleasant story in a newspaper. In short, the selectors have delegated the selection process to the tabloid newspapers.

Well, people argue, Gatting has damaged the image of the game. I cannot tell you how sick I am of the notion of image. 'Image' is an advertising word: it means a superficial appearance. What has 'image' to do with people making sane, considered judgements?

It seems that Gatting was sacked for his damage to the superficial appearance of cricket. In his stead we have

Emburey as captain and, in a bizarre step for a home series, we have Gooch appointed as his vice-captain. Both are fine cricketers but that is not the point at issue. Doubtless both are good for the image of the game. But I think the selectors have memories about as long as those of tabloid newspaper reporters.

For Emburey and Gooch are not as straightforward and bluff as they seem. They were both involved in that pattern of lies and deception that led to the rebel tour of South Africa in 1982. Gooch was captain. The tour was made in defiance of the wishes of England cricket. It made everyone involved a great deal of money, courtesy of South African Breweries. And it gave a great deal of comfort to the apartheid regime, which is exactly what it was supposed to do. The rebels were banned from international cricket for three years, which is not something I will quarrel with now. Let us say that they did their porridge and were selected back on merit as players.

But the selectors never tire of reminding us that to be England captain is to hold the highest honour in the game. And the England captain must be a man above reproach. This, presumably, is why Gatting was sacked. The appointment in his place of two men who sold English cricket down the river does not strike me as a spectacular improvement.

The selectors have adopted the moral judgements of a tabloid newspaper: sex is what matters and who cares about the politics? They have also adopted all the profound morality of an advertising agency: all that matters is the image – never mind the reality. It is true that Gatting's late night damaged the image of the game. But the actions of Emburey and Gooch damaged the heart and soul of international cricket. They were appointed as captain and vice-captain of England on Nelson Mandela's birthday.

From the Diary

Once upon a time, to be captain of England was to hold the highest honour in cricket. Now the appointment is the equivalent of being handed the pinless grenade. Every England side these days is littered with past and future captains, though at this stage of the second Test we don't know which unfortunate will get the job next. Twice in recent years England played with no fewer than seven past, present and future captains in the team. In the fourth and fifth summer Tests of 1981, England played Boycott, Brearley (the actual captain), Gower, Gatting, Botham, Emburey and Willis. Gooch, current vice-captain and former captain of England's rebel South African Breweries XI, also played. And the following winter, the seven-captain figure was reached again, with the difference that the captaincy itself had changed hands, with Fletcher replacing Brearley.

However, this is not quite a record. The Pakistanis once fielded a team with eight captains, against New Zealand in 1976. They were Majid Khan, Zaheer Abbas, Mushtaq Mohammed, Javed Miandad, Asif Iqbal, Intikhab Alam, Imran Khan and Wasim Bari. The moral is that uneasy lies the head that bears the crown – no matter how early it is laid on the pillow.

(*Note*: Gooch was later made England captain, which brings the total to a record-equalling eight.)

American sport, and American athletes, have unending problems with drugs. As chance would have it, I was in New York when Lawrence Taylor, a long-term American love-object, was caught with cocaine in his system.

SPORTING HERO FINDS CRUEL SIDE OF SUCCESS
September 1988

New York: An American hero fell from grace this week. He joined a long tradition. Heroes fall from grace all over the world: it is part of the eternal pattern of things. But when a sporting hero falls from grace in America, you can see the splash for miles.

Lawrence Taylor is that hero. A football player: linebacker for the New York Giants, and probably the finest defensive player in the history of the game: speed, mobility, improvisation, intuition – that is what characterises his game. That, and awesome destructiveness. 'I feel my way into the quarterback's skin so that I almost know his moves before he does,' Taylor said.

A great player, then. This week he failed a 'substance' test – for the second time. He is out for the first four games of the season, which starts tomorrow, and if he strays – gets caught, that is – again, he will be out of the game for life. He has admitted the substance in question was cocaine, that he has been a user for six years and an addict since 1985. 'I'm worried about what's going to happen to the rest of my life unless I get straightened out,' he said this week.

He is a man who has lived with his own gorgeous image for years. Naturally he has come to believe in it. He trumpeted forth, in his book *LT: Living On The Edge*: 'I live my life in the fast lane – and always have. I drink too much, I party too much, I drive too fast, and I'm hell on quarterbacks. It's always been that way. When someone calls me crazy, I take it as a compliment.' I fancy these are the words that Taylor would once have liked on his tombstone: he is the perfect example of a certain type of sporting hero.

It makes great copy, stuff like this. Other remarks of his are more worrying: 'A friend of mine once asked me about my driving habits. I told him I didn't wear seat belts because at the speed I go, I wouldn't survive anyway. I tell the truth: that I knew about the dangers drinking and driving brought other people. But if I don't care what happens to me, can I really think about what might happen to others?'

He occasionally reflects on death in his book: 'A long time ago I read a poem about an athlete dying young – I don't know who wrote it, but I remember feeling that if you ever did die young, when everything was going really well, that wouldn't be so bad. It would be better than growing old and watching the flowers grow.'

There are unique pressures on a footballer. Any pro athlete is under pressure all the time, but football brings this more than any other sport. The game has a uniquely high profile, and a uniquely intimate relationship with television. What is more, the sport is uniquely terrible. It is certainly the most terrible team game ever invented. Veteran players throw up from fright before games: every game has an audience of millions, every game sees the players risk appalling injuries. For the big names, the pressures increase geometrically, along with the public expectations. It is a mad and frightening game: the players lead a mad and frightening existence, and the spectacle they produce can be uniquely wonderful.

Taylor wrote: 'The thing about cocaine is that it doesn't affect you quite the same way over a long period of time. The more you use it, the more those subtle changes continue. I started to need that quietness. I could feel mellow and unhurried.'

He was caught by a drugs test two years ago, and went into 'rehabilitation'. But, still believing in his own mean sonu-vabitch image, he found the process impossible. He roared at a few people, and walked out. He cured himself, he said, by playing golf. 'The golf course was my detox tank,' he wrote. 'My therapy – not recommended for anyone else – was to enjoy myself as much as I could, to live, not like a sick or confined person – which the books and the theories tell you you should when you're addicted – but like a healthy person, able to make choices, in relative peace and freedom.'

With the benefit of hindsight, the self-deception here is painful. 'I wanted to say I could make it happen on my own,' he said sadly this week. 'I got into this mess, I could get out of it. It didn't work like that. Boy, I found that out.'

What is astonishing about Taylor's case is not that he fell from grace, but that he managed to maintain his stratospheri-cally high level of performance. It is remarkable: but it is not unusual. That people under pressure seek ease in drink and drugs is nothing new. That some athletes under pressure seek their comforts in powders and bottles is, in its way, inevitable: just as it is inevitable in my own profession.

There is a type of addict that can always function, despite the substances. Frighteningly drunk day after day, he can appear sober, do his work with competence, perhaps even with some flair. To remain employed is to maintain access to the next bottle: more often than you would think possible, an addict can learn to cope. To an extent.

And as long as he can maintain, no one knows, no one cares. A blind eye is turned: oh *he's* all right, likes his drink, but who doesn't, there's no problem there, he never misses a deadline/tackle/whatever – when he does that, we'll know there's something wrong, but right now everything's *fine*. Thus the addict is helped, even tacitly encouraged to maintain his addiction. If his performance is important to the team, nothing else matters. The addict, secretive and self-deceiving, rides that wave just as far as he can.

Taylor wrote of a terrible early binge: 'Here was a preview of my game – wildness on the field and wildness off it – success right on the edge of things. One step this way, glory. One step the other – forget it! I've been trying to keep the two in balance ever since.'

He has been encouraged by the nature of the game, the nature of the public and media interest in him, the nature of his image and his self-image, the nature of his own headlong flight from anonymity. Thus the meanest sonuvabitch who ever played football became a victim.

The nature of sporting life throws people and issues into focus with exaggerated clarity. The story of Lawrence Taylor is not a cautionary tale about sport or America: it is a story of secret addiction, and how the world conspired to keep the addiction secret – and the addict addicted. Oh, *he's* all right.

This was my first Olympic Games. It was an enormous experience, intense, unrelenting, bizarre, absurd and, for a sportswriter, an unending source of stimulation. You were never short of things to write about, that's for sure. Here are a few of the pieces I filed from Seoul.

YOU'VE RUN (AND JUMPED AND THROWN) A LONG WAY, BABY
September.1988

It is Mary Decker's teeth I hate the most. She seems to have dedicated her life to the task of turning herself into an idealised fictional version of herself: Soap Opera Woman, *Dallas* Woman, Jogging Shoe Commercial Woman, Tooth-paste Commercial Woman. The teeth get me every time. Mary Decker Slaney stands as sport's greatest living tribute to the mysteries of American orthodontistry, or tooth sculpting.

American girls spend most of their teenage years with their teeth in braces. Ostensibly, this is because of the demands of tooth sculpting, but I believe the tooth brace has been encouraged by American fatherhood as the all-American chastity belt. The tooth brace is a last-ditch attempt to postpone the transformation of girl into woman or of father into grandfather.

The end result – in a purely teeth sense – is the extraordinary vacuous look of the classic American beauty. The teeth become so large, so strong, so altogether horselike, that the mouth seems unable to close properly over them. Standard American pulchritude now involves permanently parted lips that reveal teeth like piano keys. A full smile is like an invitation to play the Emperor Concerto.

It is this – this groomed and sculptured fascia – that makes me so nervous about Mary Decker. She seems to have been designed – custom-built – as the all-American, all-feminine female sporting dame, with all that that might sell. This is something I find hard to trust.

Regardless of what might happen here at the Seoul Olympics, Mary Decker was the face of the 1984 Games, the Los Angeles Festival of American Victory. A shame that Zola Budd's ad libbing spoilt her script. But no matter what she does this time around, she will be joined, if not eclipsed, by a great band of female athletes. These Games are bringing us the biggest, most monstrous regiment of female miracle workers that sport has ever produced.

I have a feeling that these Olympics could turn into a breakthrough for all women's events. In Los Angeles, we had more women's events than ever before. But then we lacked the women to contest them. There is no such lack this time around.

Let us not forget that this is the first proper Olympics since 1972. African, American-led and Russian-led boycotts have spoiled each subsequent Olympics. This time, we have the events, and we have the women: I am sure that these Games will be, to use an expression I have never really understood but which sounds right, a watershed for women's sport. I hope that means a good thing.

I have read that women's sport is a pale imitation of the real thing. If ever there was a counter-argument to such a ludicrous statement, it is to be found in another double-barrelled American, Florence Griffith Joyner. With Mary Decker, I always feel uneasy about her double-game, her need to imply with every gesture that she's not just a great runner, she's one helluva gorgeous chick as well. Griffith Joyner does not fall into this category: she blows the whole category apart.

You might just remember her from the ranks of successful, glossy, black and comely American female athletes of 1984. By the standards of those Games, she was a kind of superior also-ran: but she was not happy about that. Even then, she was clearly a lady who could stand anything except anonymity. She was the sprinter who had to start on her knuckles because of her ludicrous nails. They were two inches long, and lacquered in red, white and blue – a change from her usual nicely understated rhinestone encrustations. I do not believe that two-inch nails are a sign of vanity. Anyone who can grow – and live with – such a preposterous and crippling affectation must possess a degree of self-absorption that would be considered unusual even in a man. It takes a male bodybuilder, a male marathon runner (a male writer?) to challenge her.

Griffith Joyner is especially enjoyable as a spectacle because her taste is so clearly theatrical, rather than merely glamorous. No one wishing to make an impression on glamour alone would try racing in a hooded speed skating suit. That extraordinary pair of one-legged combinations so perilously spread about her as she took the women's 100 metres record into the next century (is that another watershed?) was not a go-faster suit, or a practical suit, or a glamorous suit. It was a simple, straightforward, for-God's-sake-look-at-me suit. It made everyone's week, and I hope she works a further miracle here, even though she has to run in the more routine official dress of the American team: if sport cannot be ridiculous and wonderful, then there's little point to it.

But, in the end, it is not the presentation that will count in Seoul. It is the doing of it that matters. The Olympics are all about the pursuit of excellence, along with competitiveness, achievement, defiance of pain, teamwork, exuberance, the readiness to push back frontiers: all things that have been female qualities since the world began. It is just that they are not the qualities that have been most often celebrated.

For it happens to be true that women are tougher than men. Physically. They can stand the cold better, they can take extremes of heat better, their powers of endurance are far greater. They can tolerate more pain, and their balance is much better. True, men beat women at all events in track and field athletics, but as Craig Sharp, director of the human motor performance laboratory at Birmingham University, demonstrates, this is not because the events are too tough. It is because they are not tough enough.

The tougher they get, the more the gap closes. And at the preposterous end of unbelievable records and impossible challenges, women start to overtake men: in things like ultra-ultra distance swimming and trans-Himalayan running, men labour in the wake of women.

So I won't listen to anyone who would denigrate women's sport. I hope the Olympics turn out to be a giant leap forward for sports-womankind. If we seek giant leaps, then we have Sara Simeoni, the Italian high jumper, to provide them. If we seek patriotic gold medal hopes, we have Liz McColgan and Ginny Leng. We have, injuries permitting, the two British javelin throwers.

All in all, Seoul will provide the greatest festival of women's sport in the history of the world. To virtually all of this, I am happy to give the loudest possible cheer. But there are some sports, the flirting-with-the-judges kind of sports, the double-standard sports, the sports that demand gorgeousness as well as talent, that provide a further extension of the Mary Decker Problem.

Women's gymnastics can be stunning and brilliant, but the flirting by numbers that is a *de rigueur* part of the floor exercise leaves a bit of a funny taste. The graceful writhing of rhythmic gymnastics – the sport with the ribbon-waving and hoop-twirling – is also hard to be comfortable with.

There is a cigarette commercial that says to women: 'You've come a long way, baby.' These Olympics will, I hope, be a grand celebration of that fact. But I wish it were not necessary to celebrate with synchronised swimming.

HOPING FOR AN END TO
THE HUSH-UP ERA
September 1988

The men's 100 metres sprint was one of the most amazing races in Olympic history. As Ben Johnson stormed ahead with that unbelievable surge of power, leaving Carl Lewis stunned and the rest of the world inspired, surely we all thought: 'Now the Olympics have truly come alive. This is what the Olympics are all about.'

Now, with the news that Johnson has failed a dope test, we are left bewildered. The bubbles have gone out of our memories of the race, and the Olympic Games have gone joyless and flat. What is the point of stopping up half the night to watch races if the mightiest racer of them all needs chemicals to do the business?

Drugs, we agree, are bad because they are a form of cheating, and bad because they do hideous things to the people who take them. Apparently the drug for which Johnson was caught can cause cancer of the liver. But the great, almost out-of-proportion revulsion we feel against the use of performance-enhancing drugs in sport comes from somewhere deeper than rationality. We feel that there is something deeply and horribly *wrong* about drug-dependent performances.

Such events as the Olympic Games celebrate human things: triumph, despair, speed, ability, strength, grace. We want heroes: sport supplies them. We want athletes to be admirable human beings, if possible. We revel in hearing how an athlete conquers an injury and wins, or how a champion is dethroned by a brilliant youngster, or in how the old champion somehow screws out a last hurrah. These are the standard sports stories of such things as the Games, and we love to read them or even write them. They are stories about people: celebrations of human qualities.

But the drugs business takes things beyond and away from the human side of things. When athletes inject human growth hormone and bearded ladies compete for the mastery, we are no longer talking about humans. Who cares about a contest between chemists, a race between pharmaceutical freaks? Where will it all end: what new and better drugs does it take to beat Johnson? With drugged competitors, the point of the sporting event is lost. We don't want to watch it, we don't want to be associated with it. It just doesn't feel right any more.

Of course, one's second reaction, after that of bewilderment, is to feel desperately sorry for Johnson. His life is ruined. In a couple of days, he has moved from super-hero to a stuttering man with a shameful story to hide. On his grave will be written: The One Who Got Found Out. But in a twisted sort of way, one is glad; glad that at last someone of real stature has been caught. The public reaction of dismay, that such a one as this should be at it, must, one hopes, prompt the sport into action.

For in the past few months we have been shown that drugs permeate athletics from the top to the bottom. You cannot get higher than Johnson. You could not get much lower, in international terms, than poor Jeff Gutteridge, the British pole vaulter who was tested positive: he demonstrated that athletes take drugs simply to hold their own; simply to compete; simply to be there. For some – how many? – drugs seem not the last but the first resort: a necessary part of the game. Inflation has set in and is now rampant.

With Johnson, of all people, being caught, it seems we can forget the line about the 'small minority of abusers.' The problem is clearly rife, and for people all over the world, the sport will not be the same. People will turn away from athletics: they will stop watching it, they will stop sponsoring it, and they will stop their sons and daughters doing it.

The age of shamateurism was full of a million rumours of official connivance and official blind eyes. It is the same today with dope. Let us hope that with the fall of Johnson, the end of the era of the hush-up is at hand.

LOUGANIS SHINES BRIGHT ON SEOUL'S DAY OF GLOOM

September 1988

Ben Johnson was in his aeroplane at the time, pondering on the horrors of life. Back on the ground in Seoul, people were throwing up their hands and despairing about the future of the Olympic movement in the wake of the scandal. It was a day of disgrace, horror and shame. But in one small corner, it was possible to find honour, glory, graciousness and grace. It was a place where people were saying: surely, with Johnson disgraced, this is the man of the Olympics, the true Olympian, the real hero of the Games.

The place was the Olympic diving pool, and the man was Greg Louganis. He is American, so he calls himself Lougay-nis. He used the occasion to demonstrate that he is a magnificent diver, and he is a truly great competitor. He has won two gold medals, and by rights should have dropped out of the Games before getting one. His double is a triumph of mental and physical courage. It was a day on which a triumph such as this came very cheeringly.

This is a frighteningly dangerous sport. A diver aims his flight as close to the board as he dares. A couple of years ago, a Soviet hit his head attempting a dive from the 10-metre platform. He was dead before he hit the water. Last week, Louganis hit his head on the springboard in the qualifying rounds. He needed three stitches in the wound, refused pain-killers, for fear they would affect his balance, and then, serene and untroubled as you please, he won his first gold.

Louganis wants to be a film star. Well, he would, wouldn't he? In the platform final on Tuesday morning – just right for American prime-time television – one wondered about the script he was acting out. Louganis is 28, and this is his last international competition. Going into the last round, he was three points behind a 14-year-old boy from China, the amazing Xiong Ni. Xiong went first and threw in a real beauty, a dive that put Louganis out of contention, or so we thought.

Louganis stepped on to the platform. 'I thought, well, whatever happens, my mother will still love me,' he said afterwards. He stood poised, in the crucifix position, to take his farewell dive, and it was an absolute cracker. Rip entry, as American jargon has it. He won the gold by 1.14 points; by as small a margin as you could wish. Thus ended three hours of enthralling competition. Louganis said of the 14-year-old: 'He is so talented, so tough to beat. I'm really looking forward to watching his growth and development.'

Xiong said: 'It is an honour to compete with Greg Louganis. I am proud to stand beside him. He has always been my idol.' With wonderful sport and immaculate sportsmanship, it was just like being at the Olympic Games, if you see what I mean.

And now Louganis heads for the world of films. This has been an extraordinary two weeks for him. For a start, he has spent most of the time in his room, a lot of it nursing his sore head. 'I've been kind of hard on myself since I've been here,' he said. He hates to watch the Games on television because seeing

209

all those medals being won makes him restless. He doesn't like walking about the Village because he gets 'mobbed'. He has mostly sat about by himself reading film scripts: there is talk of him playing a gigolo, and naturally there is talk about a remake of Tarzan: Louganis in the paw-prints of that other Olympian, Johnny Weismuller.

In fact, there is an American Express advert running in all the right magazines in the States, which shows Louganis clad in a loincloth. I have no doubt that Louganis will do nicely. Nor can one begrudge it him in the slightest. True, he is the least bit smarmy, but let us put that down to the cultural divide. He won brilliantly, graciously, spectacularly. On a day like yesterday, it was something to be thankful for.

NOSE-CLIPS APART, SYNCHRO IS WORTH ITS WEIGHT IN GOLD
October 1988

I was there. Canada won its first gold medal of the Games – no, not the 100 metres with Ben Johnson. As you may have heard, something went wrong with that one. The first Canadian gold medal winner of the Games was Carolyn Waldo. The sport was synchronised swimming.

'I'm kind of a numb-brain, I guess you could say,' she said afterwards, when asked to explain her unearthly calm before the ordeal of subaquatic performance under gold medal pressure.

How wonderful it was to see synchronised swimming again. It has been four years since the sport was first presented to us in Los Angeles. Surely no sport can ever have made so dramatic an entrance into the national consciousness. It has become as much a figure of speech as the painting of the Forth Bridge. 'It was a bit like synchronised swimming, really,' people say, describing such things as Covent Garden, embarrassing linguistic encounters, or exchanges of over-much goodwill between politicians.

But in truth I had forgotten just how funny the sport is. 'I rolled in my seat' – *The Times*. 'I laughed and laughed' – *The*

Guardian (the man next to me). What an unmitigated treat it all was. To spend an evening simply roaring with laughter: these Games have not always been full of such things. But you can rely on synchro.

The sport is simultaneously the most showbizzy of them all, and the worst spectator sport in the history of the world. Archery? Fencing? Bags of fun. All you see at synchro is the intermittent flash of legs and the occasional extraordinary sight of a (excuse me, ladies) sequined crotch shooting ceilingwards.

'I just went in there and went for it,' Waldo said afterwards. Another thing about synchro is that it is held in an Olympic swimming pool: there are few things as brutally functional as a steel-blue, 10-lane, 50-metre pool. Synchro should be held in a heart-shaped pool lined in pink.

Of course, for insiders the sport is frightfully serious. It is frightfully difficult, too. The competitors (athletes?) train for hours every day, they pump iron, they pound out lengths. I saw Tracie Ruiz Conforto, the silver medal winner from the United States, hold her breath for two and a half minutes on the telly. The thing that baffles me is that it was Monique Berlioux, former executive director of the International Olympic Committee, and one of the most powerful ladies you could wish to meet, who invented the sport, and fought to squeeze it into the Olympics.

But enough. It is all too easy to make fun of synchronised swimming, and so I have. In sober truth, I think synchro has a real and important role to play at the Olympics. The sport has a certain dedicated and fanatical following. But that is not the real reason. The point of synchro is that it puts the entire Olympic Games in perspective.

The great danger with sport is to get swept up in it and to take the whole thing with deadly seriousness. Sport becomes a war and a religion in one if you are not careful: sport, the idiot's crusade. But sport in itself is a basically ludicrous activity. Not just the obvious lunatic fringe sports like synchro, or race walking, or the grovel-and-grope of Olympic wrestling, or the slow bicycle races. All sports are basically pointless in themselves.

Sport does have a point when people try their guts out to win them. I love the stuff. But in the cosmic scale of things, there is no real point in kicking a ball about a field, lifting up lumps of metal, or charging round and round in circles.

Sport's own self-importance makes a sense of proportion difficult to hold onto. The Olympic Games sets itself up as one of the most portentous events in the history of the world. But with synchro, we can relax. No one can be under any serious illusion that the future of the universe hangs in the balance when synchro swimmers meet in battle.

A synchro gold medal is worth exactly the same as a medal in weight-lifting, or boxing, or for that matter, the 100 metres. Every athlete, and every spectator should bear this in mind in his moment of triumph. If Steve Cram wins a gold medal today, he can say to himself: 'I have just proved myself every bit as good and every bit as important a person in the history of the universe as Carolyn Waldo, winner of the individual synchro gold.'

Long live sensible, human perspective in sport, say I. Long live synchro.

SEOUL'S VARIETY OVERWHELMS AN EMPTY FEELING
October 1988

That was my first Olympic Games, and this is my 29th piece from Seoul. In 16 days I have written about 14 sports, two or three of them for the first time. I have had an easy time of it, compared with my newswriting colleagues but, nevertheless, I am knackered.

And, of course, I wouldn't have been anywhere else in the world. As Ken Kesey's Merry Pranksters said in the 1960s, you're either on the bus or you're not on the bus. And I was on it this time. But sitting here in the Village, with all the conversation about flights home ('You're via *Seattle*?'), it is hard to get it all into perspective. Already that first Press conference – the one in which a BBC woman broke Malcolm Cooper's rifle – seems an infinitely distant experience.

If you travel a lot, you find that many places and sights are a mild disappointment: they seem somehow smaller and less imposing than they had been in your imagination. A few, a very few, are infinitely greater: the temples of Kyoto, the Taj Mahal, the ruined Burmese city of Pagan. I put the Olympics in the same class.

The sheer immensity of the Games does not come over on television. Television naturally concentrates on sports with a British interest. That represents one one-hundred-sixtieth of the Games. What about the wrestling or the Korean archers? What about the Chinese ping-pong men, the disastrous American basketball team or the one-armed baseball pitcher? Or the ferocious Korean handballers, who seem never to have been off the television here?

Above all, television concentrates on track and field, and so it should. But the Koreans do not care overmuch for athletics: that gives one a topsy-turvy sense of perspective. There was a weird sense of emptiness about the events in the athletics stadium. Last Saturday they bused in thousands of schoolkids to fill the empty seats.

The Games are about winning, and I shall remember from these Games a sense of inner deadness in those about to be winners. The dead-eyed calm of Florence Griffith Joyner in her pre-Games Press conference, the centred opacity in the face of Steve Redgrave after the first day of the rowing: these, you knew, would win gold.

Compare and contrast with the eyes of the delightful Elvis Gordon, the judo fighter, or with the gallant British women's hockey team – or with Carl Lewis. Three times during that fateful 100 metres, you saw his eyes slither uncontrollably right to Ben Johnson.

The award for the biggest nonsense is a straight fight between the pandemonium and idiocy of the boxing ring, and the sheer pointlessness of the tennis tournament.

Those events that have my jaw dropping in amazement have been the men's gymnastics, in particular the triple back-somersault performed on the floor, and the eye-cheating speed of the ping-pongers.

Awards for bravery go (inevitably) to Ginny Leng and Ian

Stark, for their brilliant rides across country, on a course that Mark Todd magnificently reduced to a gentle stroll. But the individual citation for bravery goes to Greg Louganis, the American diver who cracked his head on the springboard, and retained his nerve and composure to win two golds.

But as ever it is track and field that takes and seizes the mind at the Olympics. The greatest performance I saw was that of John Ngugi, the Kenyan winner of the 5,000 metres. That is what the Olympics should be about: African runners with wonderful faces simply running away from the finest athletes in the world. This is how fast I can run, boys; how fast can you run?

But in the end, it is that 100 metres that will remain longest in the memory. That explosion of power, that triumphant final two strides with the finger lofted in triumph: Ben Johnson, number one, no question. And then came the rather sad Press conference after the race, which reduced the hero to a lost-looking man with a stammer, not over-smart, and hating every second of the really-pretty-friendly questioning. Where would he be, I wondered, if not for athletics?

The rest of the story we all know. Never has there been such a rush to condemn a sportsman: those people and politicians who love to be photographed with successful athletes have trampled each other to death in the rush to condemn him, as if the vilifying of one man makes the rest of the sport, and the rest of the world, clean.

But condemnation comes far, far too late for athletics. For ever after, there will be a nudge-nudge and a wink-wink every time a record is shattered, or an athlete leaps dramatically forward into the big time. Drug-taking will always be on everybody's mind: I hope very much that the Johnson affair will force the sport to rid itself of drugs, and the temptation, almost the necessity, to employ them. For it is certain that unless this happens, the sport will never look the same again.

Ben Johnson left the Games as hero and victim: a victim of the world's desire for heroes, for victory, for superhuman performance. Ben Johnson is my man of the Games. My heart goes out to him.

From the Diary

With summer after summer of remorseless excellence, it has at last come to pass: a member of my own cricket team, the mighty Tewin Irregulars, has finally won international honours. Let us salute Richard Cunningham, who played for us on a single occasion a few years back, and in the great Tewin Irregulars tradition, once played against us for the British Council. He has just become a full international cricketer by playing for Czechoslovakia against Poland.

The match took place in Warsaw, and Poland won by five wickets after bowling Czechoslovakia out for 52 (Cunningham 4). But then the Czech star player, an American, was refused a visa: ah, sport is a cruel business when you reach international level.

The Czech side comprised mainly embassy Brits and Indians, and they play most of their non-international games on a very dodgy wicket in the middle of a rugby field. Already there are plans next year for a Warsaw Pact cricket tournament. All who have played for the mighty Irregulars will be cheering Czechoslovakia on.

This was an end of the sporting year piece: the enduring memory of 1988. I might have gone for some memory of sporting glory, achievement and joy, but I didn't. Instead, I found myself writing about an awkward, ambivalent moral problem, and about a deeply ambiguous figure. Such things are the stuff of sport, are they not? It makes a rather sweet-and-sour dish with which to end this collection of fish and chip wrappers, but that's sport for you. Sport may be the stuff of dreams: it is also the stuff of nightmares. All human life is there; isn't that why people read about it? And write about it?

BEN JOHNSON: A MOMENT TO REJOICE

December 1988

What was the most memorable sporting moment of 1988? There is no competition. It was the moment Ben Johnson's runaway lorry momentum broke, and he raised his right hand above his head, index finger pointing to heaven. Ben Johnson, numero uno: the greatest sprinter the world has known. In that one moment, he stood for all the joy of human life: aspiration, achievement, glory, thankfulness, utter, utter fulfilment.

You did not envy him: you rejoiced with him and for him. It was an incandescent moment, a triumph of the human spirit. All of us who were there left the stadium feeling twice as alive as before. All that is good, all that is most worthwhile about sport was celebrated in that magnificent victory, those two final, floating strides with the finger upraised for all time: numero uno. No question.

And then to the Press conference. Johnson did not come, not for hours. We heard later that he was trying to wriggle out of it, that powerful men were trying every known form of persuasion to make him step out and speak to the world's Press. The Games and, of course, the world's Press had a vested interest in the success of Johnson – it was heroics like this that we had come for.

Perhaps Johnson did not want to spoil his day of triumph. He knew the conference would be a great falling-off: he lacks all-American self-assurance, he has a stutter, he is inarticulate. No doubt he sees all kinds of hostility in the ocean of white faces that greets him on these occasions. In the end, he went through with it. Told us pretty well nothing. And that was it: off we went to write our tales of triumph.

Well, we know the rest of the story. How the race turned into a kind of modern morality play. Those who had sought to praise Johnson now sought to buy him. The politicians who would kill to be photographed next to a famous sportsman were now competing for the chance to dance on the grave of Johnson's reputation. He had disgraced his country, he had disgraced the Olympics. He was the wickedest man in the

216

history of sport. Johnson was made to stand for everything bad in the Olympics, in sport, in the whole world. Why?

Well, he cheated. But a lot of people get caught cheating in one way and another, and they don't get vilified quite like that. And legion upon legion of sportsmen take drugs: track and field stinks with the stuff, weight-lifting is putrescent with it. American football is full of mad, aggressive, steroid-crunching monsters. Lawrence Taylor of the New York Giants has been busted for cocaine twice – and he is a national hero.

But Taylor is a heroic *bad* guy. 'I drink too much, I party too much, and I'm hell on quarterbacks,' he says with pride. The cocaine fits in there quite comfortably. We want Olympians to be good guys: we wanted Johnson to be a noble athlete, bringing us chariots of fire. He was a victim of our disappointment.

Drugs make us all particularly uneasy. The innocent-seeming substance that changes you completely: this has been part of myth throughout history. Odysseus, Queen Gertrude, Alice and Dr Jekyll all had troublesome experiences with food and drink.

Added to this is a kind of squeamishness: the awful thought of doing yourself irrevocable harm. The grotesque effects various substances are supposed to have on your sexual parts are, inevitably, the most famous things about these performance-enhancing drugs; this sums up perfectly the real nature of this fear of outlandish substances. The absolute horror that drug abuse inspires is not moral, but atavistic.

Johnson is paying the bill for this. He will pay the price throughout his life, every time he thinks of what he has lost in terms of money or in terms of his hero's status. He will doubtless also pay in physical terms for what he has put his body through.

Yet Peter Elliott is a hero, and he competed in the Olympics stuffed full of pain-killers. He is a hero because of it, and I certainly would never treat a horse of mine like that. Elliott's drugging is somehow acceptable legally and morally, if not logically.

Television has made sport one of the most desirable

commodities in the world. Money, power and corruption now surround the innocent activities of playing ball and running races. Johnson has been cast as the ultimate villain in all this, but he is no villain. He is the ultimate hero, and the ultimate victim, of this sporting year.